Chambers
Cryptic Crosswords
and How to Solve Them

Michael Kindred & Derrick Knight

Chambers

CHAMBERS
An imprint of Chambers Harrap Publishers Ltd
7 Hopetoun Crescent
Edinburgh EH7 4AY

www.chambers.co.uk

This edition first published by Chambers Harrap Publishers Ltd 2002
Reprinted 2005, 2007
First edition W & R Chambers 1993

A CIP catalogue record for this book is available from the British Library.

ISBN 978 0550 10053 5

Senior Editor
Una McGovern

Consultant Editor
Catherine Schwarz

Prepress
Marina Karapanovic

Designed and typeset by Chambers Harrap Publishers Ltd, Edinburgh
Printed and bound in Great Britain by Cox & Wyman Ltd, Reading, Berkshire

Preface

This book, which is the result of a long collaboration between Michael and myself, had its origin in the discovery one Sunday morning that we both enjoyed the intriguing world of cryptic crosswords.

During the week which followed, I set a puzzle for Michael; he soon solved it and retaliated. This led to our setting puzzles for each other and offering constructive criticism on how they might be improved. The setting of mine was a pleasant means of whiling away my daily train journey to London. I was interrupted quite often by fellow-commuters who wanted me to explain various clues in most of the daily newspapers. Thus the idea for this book emerged. The gestation period saw many changes from the original concept to what was sent to the publisher, together with many changes from that manuscript to the first edition.

Since then, we have developed our skills, and this is hopefully reflected in the many changes incorporated in this revised edition. We have also entered the world of advanced cryptic crosswords, an introduction to which is now included. Through this I met Georgie Johnson with whom I have collaborated on one of the themed crosswords.

I am indebted to my uncle, the late Bill Burdett, for my two lifelong passions of cricket and crosswords. Michael's first mentor was his grandmother, the late Eneata Holman, on whose knee he sat many a time, generally hindering progress towards completion of the puzzles.

Derrick Knight

Contents

Introduction

Cryptic Crosswords and How to Solve Them is designed to teach all the cryptic tricks of the trade through a series of graded puzzles with clues to the clues. We have deliberately kept formal instruction to a minimum since one of the ideas behind this book is the belief that people enjoy actually doing crosswords rather than reading about how to do them. It is also true to say that most people probably learn how to solve cryptic crosswords in exactly the sort of way that we have set out to demonstrate here: by studying the solutions and working back through the clues.

This process of induction usually happens in two ways. The dedicated and self-reliant learner will often build up familiarity with clue types by the simple expedient of solving what he or she can, and then trying to work out the structure of the remaining clues by reference to the solution grid when it appears. More commonly, a friend, relative or colleague will introduce a beginner to the joys of solving by providing background information to the various clue types. Practice and enthusiasm gradually produce increased speed and efficiency, and enable the novice to progress to more complicated puzzles. Most people begin solving crosswords through a combination of the two routes described above.

What we have sought to do in this book is to provide a more formal model of this kind of informal familiarization and training process — laid out in a way that provides solvers not only with a programmed learning approach, but with a convenient source of reference to clue types, abbreviations and many of the arcane instruments of the crossword setter's art. (No wonder the two most famous setters' pseudonyms — Ximenes and Torquemada — have their origins in the tortured history of the Inquisition!)

The material is laid out in what we hope is a reasonably logical manner. First of all, we have provided a simple summary of **Cryptic Clue Types and Devices** designed to introduce the solver to all the most commonly encountered clue structures. The listing in this section is comprehensive and practical; it cannot hope to be exhaustive because crossword compilers are a devious bunch and are always trying to come up with some novel device to test the solver. Nonetheless, our summary is more than adequate as a key to the kinds of clue you will encounter in crosswords appearing in the national dailies and, needless to say, it covers all the clues featured in our own puzzles. A summary of the clue types is also printed at the back of the book: the summary is intended as a handy reference for the graded puzzles that follow, some of which contain a shorthand indication of clue type as an aid to solving.

The next section gives **Some Practical Advice on Solving**: it tackles some of the methodological and psychological aspects of solving (such as what to do when you get stuck!) as well as providing a necessarily subjective guide to the relative difficulty of a cross-section of crosswords that appear in various daily newspapers.

Now we come to the core of the book: the **Graded Puzzles**. These have been divided into three sections, each of which presents ten puzzles. The first section (Crosswords 1–10) contains the 'initiation' puzzles — those in which the beginner is offered most help. The initiation puzzles feature: partially completed grids, highlighted indications of definitional elements in the clues, shorthand keys to clue types and, as far as possible, relatively simple clues and solutions.

Crosswords 11 – 20 still retain the bracketed indications of clue types but dispense with the definitional highlighting and 'on-grid' solutions, while the final ten puzzles (Crosswords 21–30) contain no guidance other than the comprehensive explanations which appear in the relevant **Help** section preceding the **Solutions**. Some of the clues and solutions in these final puzzles are quite tough — so be warned.

In compiling the puzzles we have taken the view that most of the people who will use this book will be wanting to learn or improve their technique for solving crosswords in the 'big' dailies. Therefore, we have tried to set clues that are reasonably representative of the clue types and level of difficulty that solvers will encounter when tackling such puzzles. Since this is the case we recommend that you have available a good English dictionary. The latest edition of *The Chambers Dictionary* is comprehensive (including a lot of literary, obscure and dialect words and usages as well as covering current language) and offers good value for money.

The beginner who works through all thirty puzzles should be equipped to tackle successfully (even if slowly at first) the cryptic puzzles that appear in papers such as the *Daily Telegraph*, *The Guardian*, *The Independent* or *The Times* — the latter of which is generally acknowledged to be the most consistently challenging.

We have included in this revised edition an introduction to advanced cryptic crosswords, **Beyond the Black-and-White Grid**, hoping to demonstrate that they are far from impossible. The four **Themed Puzzles** which follow this section are examples of this level of cryptic puzzle.

As additional assistance, the book includes a **Two-way Crossword Glossary**. This is intended as no more than a summary of the most common cryptic indications, and 'crossword speak' — but it will certainly prove a useful reference source for the beginner. Those who wish to obtain more comprehensive reference works may go to the **Further Reading and Contacts** section. There are various excellent titles recommended here for those who feel themselves destined to become fanatics.

Cryptic Clue Types and Devices

The word 'cryptic' means 'mysteriously obscure, secret, hidden', and the art of setting cryptic crosswords always involves an attempt to mislead the solver in some way. In fact, the best cryptic clues are invariably those that read as apparently normal English sentences or phrases, but which actually indicate a solution that has nothing whatever to do with the obvious literal sense of the clue.

Solvers of ordinary definitional crosswords may well throw up their hands in horror at this deliberate double-speak. To the cryptic fan, however, such dissimulation is the whole essence of the challenge. An added (and perhaps surprising) feature of cryptic crosswords is that the solver usually knows immediately that a solution is correct without needing to relate it to intersecting letters of other solutions. This is because cryptic clues normally contain separate elements within them — and these elements must cross-check to produce a consistent answer.

A cryptic clue always contains a *definition* of the answer to be found together with a 'mysteriously obscure' part which, when solved, also leads to the answer. This latter part is usually referred to as the *subsidiary indication*. The definition normally comes at the beginning or end of a clue, rarely in the middle.

Example: **Bad head ailment** (7). 'Ailment' is the definition and 'bad head' is the subsidiary indication. Of course, it's not meant to be obvious when you first look at a clue which part is which: much of the fun is working that out! So, in this example, 'bad' = ILL and 'head' = NESS. Added together these give ILLNESS which is defined by 'ailment'.

It is important to examine each word in the clue to determine which is the definition and which the subsidiary indications. Setters try to make clues as tight as possible so that each word is significant. Clues must also make sense. It is therefore sometimes necessary to use *linking words* such as 'in', 'to', 'on', 'from', 'and', 'giving', 'finds', etc. You will also come across the use of the definite or indefinite article in a definition. This is in order to make the clue read better, as in 11 Across in Crossword 1. The definite or indefinite article is not however required to be part of the solution.

In the example above there is nothing which is superfluous or unnecessary as part of the clue, but in many of the puzzles in this book solvers will find linking words. Such words applied to the clue for ILLNESS might be 'producing', as in 'Bad head producing ailment' or 'from' as in 'Ailment from bad head'. A more appropriate link might be 'on' in 'Bird box on line (7)'. 'Box' = SPAR + 'line' = ROW = SPARROW, defined by 'bird'. Without 'on' the clue would not make sense.

The number in brackets at the end of a clue indicates the number of letters in the answer. You may think: 'Why bother to give that information? It's obvious when you look at the diagram'. First of all, it saves you from having to consult the diagram every time you look at a clue; secondly, it is necessary for indicating when an answer comprises more than one word or is a hyphenated word. For example (3,4) would mean that the answer is two words, the first one three letters long, the second one four letters long. If it were written (3-4), this would indicate that the word has a hyphen in it after the third letter. Many editors do not now specify a hyphen. They would show a hyphenated seven-letter word as (7), which you may not think is particularly helpful.

Now for a list of the common clue types and devices. This list is not meant to be exhaustive as there are some clue types and devices used in certain very difficult kinds of cryptic crosswords which, if included here, would make the list too cumbersome and probably frighten the life out of you at this stage! If you cope successfully with the crosswords in this book, then there are other books which will give you an insight into even deeper mysteries of cryptic clues.

The letter introducing each clue type is a reference used in the first two sets of **Graded Puzzles** (Crosswords 1–10 and Crosswords 11–20) and also in the clue type key which appears at the back of this book. To help you further, in the first ten puzzles we have highlighted the principal definitional element in many of the clues in **bold** type.

It will be seen that we have included some clueing methods which are rather dubious. This is because, although the more particular editors will ensure that they do not appear, solvers may well come across them.

a. Double or multiple definitions

Two or more definitions of the word to be found are chosen so that when they appear together they are misleading.

Examples: **Signify** low average (4) = MEAN

State proviso (9) = CONDITION

As these clues are sometimes rather difficult to solve you should not meet too many in one puzzle.

It is appropriate here to point out that it is inaccurate for any type of clue to be defined by example. **Push** pram (5) would not be a fair clue for BARGE, since 'pram' is an example of a BARGE. To make this fair the setter would need to add an indication of such: eg, say, for example, etc. It follows that spotting such indications may well lead you to the definition — but not necessarily! Definitions by example do creep in.

b. Single definition

Although the solution is a single definition, it is not a straightforward or literal definition of the words in the clue. A very old joke provides an example:

Example: What lies quivering at the bottom of the sea? (1,7,5) = A
NERVOUS WRECK

(A question mark is sometimes used to emphasize the misleading and perhaps humorous nature of a single definition, as in the above example.)

c. Anagram

i) **Simple**: The letters of one or more words in the clue are rearranged to form the answer. An *anagram indicator* also appears somewhere in the clue so that you know that some letters have to be rearranged.

Example: Grab torn **dress** (4) = GARB
'Grab' rearranged

In this example 'torn' is the anagram indicator.

Essentially an anagram indicator should signify that a rearrangement of the letters of a word or words is required. More examples of anagram indicators are given below.

(We have used the term 'simple' to enable us to use the term 'complex' for the other more difficult kinds of anagram. 'Simple' is not meant to indicate that solving the actual anagram is necessarily easy!)

ii) **Complex**: The letters of one or more words that do not actually appear in the clue have first of all to be found from a word or words in the clue. These letters then have to be rearranged to form the answer.

Example: Snatch torn **dress** (4) = GARB

The anagram is formed from a synonym of 'snatch' = grab, where 'torn' is again the anagram indicator.

A common variation occurs when part of the anagram is an abbreviation, number or symbol derived from some of the words in the clue.

Example: **Dress** made from black rag (4) = GARB
B + 'rag' rearranged

In this example 'black' = B, and the anagram indicator is 'made from'.

iii) **Subtractive**: In this type of anagram the solver is required to remove some letters from those to be rearranged to form the solution.

Example: Without ado, paradox is resolved in **a practical exercise** (6)

'Without' indicates 'ado' must be removed from 'paradox is'. 'Resolved' is the anagram indicator and a word defined as 'a practical exercise' must be formed from the remainder. 'Parxis' becomes PRAXIS.

A variation of the subtractive anagram requires jumbled letters to be removed before arriving at the solution letters.

Example: Schoolmaster leaving out complex tomes for **pupil** (7)

'Leaving out' signifies something is to be omitted. 'Complex' is the anagram indicator for 'tomes'. The letters from 'tomes' unravelled and removed from 'Schoolmaster' leave SCHOLAR = 'pupil'.

Finally, jumbled letters may need to be removed from a jumble to produce the letters from which the answer is to be formed. In this case a second anagram indicator will be used.

Example: Expelling crazy Amos, schoolmaster exploded into **laughs** (8)

'Expelling' indicates removal, 'crazy' an anagram of 'Amos' and 'exploded' an anagram of 'schoolmaster'. Therefore the letters of AMOS must be removed from those of SCHOOLMASTER, leaving 'cholster' = CHORTLES.

Examples of anagram indicators:

Anagram indicators are words which indicate the movement or rearrangement of letters, such as 'flying', 'wild', 'exploding', 'shuffle', 'shake', 'arrange', 'circulate', 'haphazard', 'unwind', 'reforming', 'twisted', 'change'. Different tenses of a word may be used, such as 'change', 'changes', 'changing', 'changed'. Many setters also now use the imperative form, as in Puzzle 7, clue 17 down.

Sometimes, less obvious words are used as anagram indicators, such as 'fancy', 'out', 'high' or even 'on' (= playing).

You will realize from this that many words can serve to indicate that the letters of another word or words in the clue are to be rearranged. In solving the puzzles in this book you will probably find that you begin to build up a mental list of some of them. Many are also featured in the **Two-way Crossword Glossary.**

d.   Split

The answer is made up of linked parts as in the party game of Charades.

Example: Interrupt quick **meal** (9) = BREAKFAST
'interrupt' = BREAK + 'quick' = FAST

The clues for AILMENT and SPARROW, above, are further examples. After anagrams, these are possibly the most popular clues with setters and solvers alike.

e.   Sandwich

One component of the answer is expressed as, for example, being 'in' or 'around' another. There are numerous ways of indicating this, such as 'held by' or 'holds', 'embracing', etc. Look out for ours. Where the simple 'in' is used, it can be misleadingly placed, as in Puzzle 7, clue 16 Down, or used imperatively. Most editors do not now allow the latter.

Example: **Commissioned** to set in action (7) = DEPUTED
PUT = 'set' in DEED = 'action'

f.   Takeaway sandwich

In this case, part of the 'filling' of a 'sandwich' is taken away to give the answer, either from words featured in the clue or from synonyms of them.

Example: **Bank** freshly releasing American currency (4) = RELY
'Freshly' = RECENTLY, less, ie 'releasing', 'American currency' =
CENT

g. Reverse direction, either horizontal or vertical

A word or words must be written either back to front in an Across clue, or
from bottom to top in a Down clue. The word or words indicating this
process usually correspond with the clue direction. For Across clues, the
indicator may be, for example, 'returning', 'back' or 'round', while for a
Down clue it could be 'rising' or 'falling', 'uplifting', or simply 'up' or 'down'.

Example: Sly look round **fortress** (4) = KEEP
'Sly look' = PEEK, which is reversed

h. Hidden word

The answer is found in the wording of the clue, and a word such as 'some' or
'part' or 'in' is used to indicate that this is so.

Example: **Try** some white streamers (4) = TEST ('whiTE STreamers')

i. Sound effects

The solution is usually a synonym of one of the elements in the clue and a
homophone of (that is, sounds like) another. Indicators of this may be, for
example, 'we hear', 'sounds like', 'said', 'reported'.

Example: **Animal** sounds husky (5) = HORSE (sounds like 'hoarse')

j. Takeaway

Part of a word is taken away, leaving the answer, rather as in *f.* above.

Example: **Design** flying machine with no tail (4) = PLAN ('flying machine'
= PLANE minus E)

k. Moving letter

One or more letters is/are directed to another position in the word.

Example: **Look**: Pepe's swallowing his tail (4) = PEEP (final 'e' from 'Pepe')

l. Substituted letter

One letter of a word in the clue takes the place of another, and there will be a
word or phrase indicating that this is so.

Example: **Value** change of direction from North (5) = WORTH

'Direction' in this clue indicates a compass direction (the solver has to
discover this), so the N = 'North' changes to W = 'West'. Although
'Value' in the clue is read as a verb, this is meant to mislead: the
definition requires 'value' to be regarded as a noun.

m. Alternate letters

The answer is produced from alternate letters in part of the clue. The
indicator for this type may be, for example, 'evenly', 'unevenly', 'oddly',
'every other', 'alternately', 'intermittently'.

Example: **Tile** uneven hearth (3) = HAT (HeArTh)

n. Letter positions

i) **Initials or last letters only**: The first or last letters of the indicated words are taken to produce the answer. 'First' or 'last' may also be used without the qualifying 'of' or 'of all', but this is inaccurate. See also *n. ii)* below.

The indicator for the first letters may be, for example, 'firstly', 'first of all', 'initially', 'heads of', 'tops of'.

Example: First of all maybe one uses new tackle to **climb** (5) = MOUNT

Take the first letters of 'Maybe One Uses New Tackle'

The indicator for the last letters may be, for example, 'ends of', 'lastly', 'last of all'.

Example: Last of all find the little river **animal** (4) = DEER

Take the last letters of 'finD thE littlE riveR'

ii) **Only specifically placed letters**: Letters in certain positions in indicated words are taken to produce part or, in a few cases, the whole of the answer.

The indicator for the first letter of a word may be similar to those in *n. i)*, except indicators in the plural would become singular: 'head of', 'top of'. Also, a word with 'head' or 'top' at the end may indicate that the first letter of that word is to be taken; for example: 'Gateshead' = G, or 'worktop' = W. These two examples are now widely regarded as inaccurate. For 'Gateshead' see *p. i)* and *p. ii)* below. 'Worktop' should be 'top of work' or at least 'work's top'.

The indicator for the middle letter of a word may be, typically, 'centre of', 'middle of', 'heart of', 'centre'. So, 'Middle of Glasgow' would be S.

The indicator of the last letter of a word might be, perhaps, 'end of', 'lastly', 'tail of'. So, 'end of sermon' would be N. Also, a word with 'end' or 'tail' at the end would indicate that the last letter of the word before 'end' or 'tail' is to be taken; for example: 'fantail' would be N. The criticism applied to 'worktop' is equally valid for this example.

The indicator for other positions could be simply 'second', 'third', 'fourth' and so on, indicating that the second, third or fourth letter of the word indicated is to be taken; for example: 'third of January' is N.

Examples of some of the above:

   Mist in the centre of Oxford fading finally (3) = FOG
   FO = 'the centre of Oxford' + the last letter of fadinG

   Reluctant 'Heart of Midlothian' (4) = LOTH

o. Abbreviations, numbers and symbols

Abbreviations are often used to indicate one or more letters in a solution.

Example: **A mass meeting** of everyone in the railway (5) = RALLY

'Everyone' = ALL in RY — which is an abbreviation of 'railway' or 'railway line'. Sometimes just the word 'line' is used to indicate the abbreviation RY. 'The' is a linking word.

Some dictionaries carry a list of common abbreviations, and a look through these will show that there is plenty scope for their use in clues. As you work through the crosswords in this book, you will gradually become familiar with many of them. Some of the more common ones, however, are worth mentioning here.

Let's start off with the points of the compass: North, South, East and West are often abbreviated to N, S, E and W respectively. In clues these are often referred to as 'points', 'quarters' or 'directions' — the latter quite possibly also being NE, SE, SW and so on. Other geographical references may well include the abbreviations of countries (US or USA and all its states — CA, PA, NY, for example) or features such as 'river' (R), 'mountain' (MT) and 'lake' (L).

Moving from places to people, we often encounter professions and qualifications such as DR, GP or MB ('doctor'), DA ('American lawyer', or just 'lawyer'), RA ('painter'), REV ('vicar', 'priest' or 'churchman'), MP, LIB, LAB, C, TORY ('Member' or 'politician') and BA or MA ('graduate'). A 'learner', by the way, is nearly always L and a 'saint' or 'good man' ST.

Abbreviations relating to the armed forces are also very common. The favourites are probably TA ('army', 'reserves' or 'volunteers'), RA ('gunners' or 'artillery'), RE ('engineers' or 'sappers') and GI (frequently just 'soldier'). The 'navy' (RN) seems to recruit mainly ABs ('sailors' when they are not TARS) and the occasional RM (very often a 'jolly' fellow) to sail aboard its 'ships' (SS), while the air force (RAF) has a full complement of ACS (usually 'airmen'). Every AC will pay wages into a 'current' (AC or DC) 'account' (again AC), of course.

Military personnel are commanded by a variety of 'officers' — both commissioned (CO) and non-commissioned (NCO) — ranging from GEN through COL, LT and CAPT to SGT, but often referred to simply as 'commanding officer' (CO) or the person 'in charge' (IC). At the head of the armed forces is the monarch — the 'king' or 'queen' — who may well be a George (GR), an Elizabeth (ER, or if 'the First', ERI), or simply an R, and who receives religious sanction from the 'Church' (CE or CH).

After the fighting is over, one of the principal forms of relaxation is cricket, in which 'runs' (R) are scored, often as 'extras' (LB or leg-byes), on both 'sides' of the 'wicket' (W) — OFF and ON/LEG, though these are not really abbreviations. In cricket, if you are not 'batting' (IN), you are out, and this can happen in a number of ways: 'caught' (C) is the most common, although many players are 'bowled' (B) and some can even be 'stumped' (ST). Golf, tennis, rowing, football (run by the FA, of course), rugby (RU) and bridge (for which 'partners', N, S, E, W are required) are other pastimes much favoured in crosswords. Team games are mostly played by an 'eleven'

(XI) or a 'fifteen' (XV); however, these belong to the realm of 'numbers' (NOS).

Not surprisingly, Roman numerals are a staple feature of cryptic crosswords. Just to remind you: I = 'one', IV = 'four', V = 'five', IX = 'nine', X = 'ten', L = 'fifty', C = 'hundred' (and is also an abbreviation for *circa* meaning 'about'), D = 'five hundred' and M = 'thousand'. Perhaps the most common number in crosswords is O, which can be indicated by 'zero', 'nought', 'none', 'no', 'nothing' and quite often by 'love' — a reference to tennis scoring.

Strictly speaking, of course, numbers are symbols rather than abbreviations. Other symbols to be 'noted' are A, B, C, D, E, F, G — musical notes, which can also crop us as DO(H), RE/RAY, MI/ME and so on. Symbols for chemical 'elements' are not uncommon, such as K (potassium), NA (sodium) and S (sulphur). X is indicated in a variety of ways: as well as being the number 'ten', it is also a 'kiss', a 'cross' and an 'unknown quantity' (for which Y may also serve).

These are just a few of the many building blocks for 'structural' clues. The **Two-way Crossword Glossary** features many more examples for reference when you start doing the puzzles.

p. Misleading punctuation

i) *Misleading marks or absence of them*: An example of this would be the use of the word 'Gateshead' in a clue to indicate G, (see *n. ii)*). 'Gates' should really have an apostrophe thus: 'Gate's'.

ii) *Running words together or falsely separating them*: (This also includes the running together or separation of a word and a letter.) Using the same example as in *p. i)*, 'Gateshead' should be two words: 'Gate's head', or the clue 'Hardback?' (5) for STERN should be read as 'Hard back'. It is then a double definition. Similarly 'Dispatch to Southend' (4) should read as 'South end'. S = an abbreviation for 'South' + END gives SEND. See also Puzzle I, clue 22 Down and Puzzle 8, clue 10 Across.

iii) *False upper or lower case letters*: Again, we can use 'Gateshead' as an example: literally, it should be 'gate's head'. In *k.* above, 'Pepe's' should be 'pepe's'. 'Amos' in the clue for CHORTLES in *c. iii)* above is a further example.

Here we may be permitted a diversion on the use of 's. This is often used for linkage as in Puzzle 3, clue 11 Across or Puzzle 11, clue 29 Across. In neither of these examples is the 's consistently correct when comparing the clue with the answer. However, it is a widely used device.

In order to be fair to solvers the preamble 'punctuation may mislead' should appear when these devices are used. For this reason some editors now prefer to avoid them.

q. Literary, historical or artistic references

Where literature is involved, references are now usually used in preference to direct quotations.

Examples: The less dignified end of one of Shakespeare's characters? (6) = BOTTOM

The Bard's small village? (6) = HAMLET

Constable's transport? (3,3,4) = THE HAY WAIN

The question mark is used to indicate the 'tongue-in-cheek' nature of these clues.

Where direct quotations are used, setters usually try to ensure that they are either well known or that they can be reasonably easily deduced from their context.

Example: 'Cry — , and let slip the dogs of war' *(Julius Caesar)* (5) = HAVOC

r. Direct or indirect reference to another clue in the puzzle, or its answer

This may be expressed in the form: 7 *Dn's* muddled thought (4) = IDEA, where the answer to the 7 Down clue is AIDE.

s. Archaic indicator

Sometimes a setter will use a word which is no longer in common usage or is an obsolete meaning of an everyday word, and it is only fair to solvers that this should be indicated in some way in the clue. Examples of these indicators are: 'ancient','old', 'was', 'Shakespearian','Spenser's'.

Example: Old penny has changed to **Mark** (4) = DASH

D + 'has' anagram

In this example, an 'old penny' is indicated by the symbol D (now largely obsolete) and 'Mark' is misleadingly printed with the upper-case 'M'.

t. Miscellaneous

Sometimes a clue, or part of a clue, doesn't fit into any of the above types.

Example: **A tiny particle** of a,b,c,d,e,f,g,h,i,j,k,l,m (4) = ATOM
(A TO M)

Where we have used such a clue it is explained in the **Help for Graded Puzzles** section.

u. Definition also being a part of, or the whole of, the device

At the beginning of this section of the book we wrote about cryptic clues containing a definition and a subsidiary indication. We now come to the type of clue where either the definition is included in part of the subsidiary indication or the subsidiary indication is also the definition.

Example: **Broken** tubs (4) = BUST

Here, 'broken' is both the definition and the anagram indicator.

Example: **Heads of** the several amalgamated **Russian States** (5) = TSARS

In this case, despite the bold type, the whole clue is effectively both the definition and the subsidiary indication. This is what is known as a true '& *lit.*' clue, which means that it offers a subsidiary indication (in this case the type *n. i)* above) and a literal definition, both of which use all the words in the clue.

You will find out more about & *lit.* clues in the following chapter, **Some Practical Advice on Solving**.

Some Practical Advice on Solving

Before you start trying to solve the crosswords in this book, just take the time to read this short section. It will give you some useful pointers to various strategies you can employ when tackling a crossword, as well as a brief run-down on the puzzles you will find in a few of the national dailies.

If you are a real beginner at cryptic crosswords, you could well benefit from the practical advice offered here — firstly to establish a sound technique, and secondly to prevent your getting overwhelmed or dispirited when you gaze at a blank grid and a lot of seemingly bizarre clues.

We recommend that, whilst remembering to have fun, you approach the task as if it were an IQ test or a multiple choice examination. If in doubt, move on and come back to the question later. It is advisable to read through all the clues in order (Across, then Down) before you begin filling in the grid. It is frustrating and pointless to struggle over, say, an Across clue when one or two easy intersecting Down clues would have provided you with useful cross-checking letters.

During this quick evaluation process try to identify the definitional element which normally comes at the beginning or the end of each clue, perhaps underlining it en route. Once you have done this, most types of clue become much more accessible. You should also look out for hidden word and anagram devices since clues containing these are usually the easiest to solve. When you find such clues, ring round the number so you can go back to them later — you're already halfway there with the solution. While you are reading the clues, you can also tick (or otherwise mark) any that you think you have solved correctly.

Having gone through the clues in this way — which shouldn't take you more than about five minutes — use a pencil (or a pen, if you are feeling confident) to write in those solutions you have worked out. Then set about unscrambling the anagrams you have identified.

Most solvers find it easiest to do anagrams by separating out the consonants and vowels of the constituent word or words. When written down in this way, the individual letters can be more easily dissociated in the mind from the form of the original clue so that attention can be focused on the various potential letter combinations of the solution indicated. It is often helpful to identify any possible consonant clusters or obvious sequences of letters (such as CH, CK, PH, QU, SH, TH, CL, THR and so on) that might form part of the rearranged solution. It is also important to relate the tense or number implied by the clue indicator to the letters in the anagram. For example, in 'Staple used to form folds (6)', the word 'folds' indicates a plural answer is to be sought (PLEATS). Or in 'Fed up by getting dates wrong (5)', where a past tense is implied by 'Fed', you can begin by working out words that can be formed with the ending -ED. (The answer is, of course, SATED). All this being said, you must still bear in mind that the plurals of many Latinate terms end in -I (especially those of plants) and that certain strong verbs in English have past forms ending in -T or -N (THOUGHT and RIDDEN for example), so don't allow your mind to shut out these possibilities. Other useful endings to look for are -ION, -ITY and -UDE (abstract nouns), -ER and -OR (often common nouns or 'agents'), -ING (verbs and verbal nouns) and -ABLE, -IBLE, -UBLE or -IOUS, -OUS (adjectives). Prefixes such as ANTE-, ANTI-, BE-, CON-, DE-, DIS-, FOR-, IN-, MIS-, RE- and UN- are also useful starting points. Finally (though there is a lot more we could say about anagrams), the letter Y is a semi-vowel, and some solvers write it down separately above the line of constituent vowels in their anagram letter listing. Y can often be used to form an adjective (PRETTY) but it just as frequently functions as a vowel on its own (SKY) or a letter modifying the sound of a preceding vowel (TRAY, GREY and so on). These comments of course apply to all possible grid entries, regardless of clue type.

Having solved one or two of the anagrams means that you will now have some letters of the intersecting answers (or *lights* or *grid entries* as they are sometimes termed). These 'check squares' will provide you with a much better basis on which to go back and review the other clues.

It is important to realize that many of the clues in cryptic crosswords contain 'structural' devices — such as the abbreviation of directions (N, E, S,W) — which are part of the final solution. To have established a little of the content of a light through a check letter can therefore be even more useful in a cryptic crossword than in an ordinary definition-only puzzle, as the letter you have may often represent a key pointer towards the construction of the clue.

Which clues should you concentrate on next? Try the longer solutions first since their component letters are clearly going to be helpful in solving the other clues, for the reason indicated above. Kind setters may of course have clued longer words with anagrams. Concentrate on one corner or area of the puzzle at a time. The more clues you solve, the easier the others will become. This is not merely because of the insights provided by the intersecting letters: it is also a method of getting to know a particular setter's mind, style and personal enthusiasms.

Make sure, however, that you don't get obsessed at an early stage with individual clues: there's plenty of time for that later! If your brain begins to overheat have a look at another clue or move to a different area of the puzzle. One of the pleasing things about crosswords of all varieties is that your mind is always working on associations and ideas, even while you are apparently concentrating on something else. It is surprising how often a seemingly opaque clue becomes obvious after a short break.

This is particularly true when you are at an early stage of learning how to do cryptic crosswords, largely because much of the learning process involves becoming attuned to the different kinds of ambiguity encountered in the clues. People who are unfamiliar with cryptic crosswords often complain that they read like a foreign language and, although there seems an element of truth in this, learning to understand the language of crosswords ('Crossword English', as described by Don Manley in *Chambers Crossword Dictionary*) is much easier than learning French, German or Latin because crosswords use terms with which we are all familiar.

In some ways solving is rather like cracking a code — a code in which, for example, a graduate is almost invariably an MA or BA, a bridge is often a SPANNER and a duck or love might be O. We have tried to list some of the more common ambiguities (mostly abbreviations and symbols) in the **Two-way Crossword Glossary**. However, there are literally thousands of potential ways of wrong-footing the solver and, taking the language-learning parallel again, it is a matter of becoming used to thinking in the language rather than learning every word of it by heart. Best expressed, the trick is to think laterally but always logically.

Pursuing this theme a little further, let us look for a moment at word order. It is vital that you do not allow the apparently innocent literal meaning of a clue to influence your judgement about the solution indicated. In many ways this is probably a bigger hurdle for the novice than the matter of learning to cope with the abbreviations, symbols and vocabulary of cryptic puzzles. You really need to approach each clue by thinking of ways in which the natural syntax could be disrupted. Take, for example, a clue from a typical *Times* crossword: 'Doctor calls back after 45 minutes (8)'. In this clue, 'calls' could be NAMES, which spelt backwards is SEMAN. This must be put 'after' three-quarters of an hour — HOU ('45 minutes') — giving you HOUSEMAN, and confirming that the first word of the clue is the definitional element. You can see from this that even the word 'after' contains a possible ambiguity since your first thought might well have been that the '45 minutes' element should actually follow 'calls back'. This is not to mention the fact that we have already made the assumption that 'Doctor' is a noun: it could quite easily have been a verb, or even an anagram indicator! The point is that you must be prepared to dissect each clue and examine every word in order to reach the correct solution.

Whilst, as mentioned above, most clues are likely to provide answers which have nothing to do with their literal meanings, setters do like to include what are called '& lits'. This means that although the clue will be made up as we indicated, the answer may be a literal meaning of the clue. One of Derrick's for the *Independent on Saturday*, a simple hidden clue, was 'Bird occupying higher nest (4)'. You should be able to find it!

Of course, not all clues are of the structural type: many depend simply on puns and *double entendres*. These clues are often the most amusing and the most satisfying to solve, although they are often the most difficult because there is no way of building up the answer. Once again, a typical example from a *Times* crossword: 'Europeans who go to Rome for religious service (5,5)'.

Apart from the implication that the solution has a plural ending, this clue depends entirely on a misreading of 'service'; once you have figured out that the connotation is a military one, the solution (SWISS GUARD) is fairly obvious. The lateral jump of the imagination needed to make this connection is what solving cryptic crosswords is all about, and to learn to think in this way takes time and practice — so don't be put off if you can't solve this sort of clue quickly: you often need to have quite a few intersecting letters before the answer becomes obvious and the pun dawns on you. It's almost a question of needing to have the solution in order to understand the clue!

In this respect, you should not be afraid of the occasional piece of inspired guesswork. Sometimes the check letters dictate that a particular solution is almost inevitable, and it is only after you have written it down that you make the connection. Even so, you are strongly advised not to ink in a solution until you are absolutely sure that you have understood why it is correct. An incorrect or hasty assumption can hold you up for an awfully long time. It is advisable just to trace the letters of a 'best guess' on any blank check squares rather than write in the whole word or phrase. Apart from anything else, writing in a suspicion that proves to be wrong makes it extremely difficult to concentrate on getting the right answer after you have realized your mistake.

Another useful point to bear in mind is that most normal puzzles will contain a fairly even balance of the different types of clue device, carefully distributed throughout the grid. In other words, there will be several anagrams, a number of structural clues, a few puns, no more than one or two hidden words and 'initial letter' clues, and perhaps a quotation. These will all be mixed into the sequence of clues so that you are unlikely to encounter a large number of consecutive clues of the same type. This factor can be particularly useful if you are stuck on a certain clue: it is quite possible that it will feature a different device from the ones immediately preceding and following it. For tuition purposes we have deviated a little from this general rule in the puzzles in this book.

Of course, different setters favour different types of clue and so the overall balance can differ from puzzle to puzzle. It is also possible for personal enthusiasms to manifest themselves within both the clues and solutions: gardening, cricket, bridge and certain periods of literature are particularly common, and, more recently, computerese. Some crosswords are deliberately constructed with particular themes or leitmotifs in mind, although this is usually made explicit in an accompanying rubric. Despite the balance and variation of clue types, however, it is probably fair to say that each of the major dailies has a certain style that characterizes most of the puzzles it features. The truth of this may be judged from the fact that once you have become used to solving puzzles in one paper, it can take you a while to get to grips with the puzzles in another — even though the level of difficulty may be similar, or perhaps even lower.

Our own experience does not allow detailed comment on the puzzles that appear in *The Scotsman* (which has an excellent crossword) or in the *Irish Times*. You may, however, be interested in a thumbnail sketch of some of those with which we are more familiar in order to plan your future newspaper order.

The *Financial Times* features a daily cryptic of medium difficulty. The clues are enjoyable, though rarely either abstruse or particularly inspired. This is an excellent proposition for the relative beginner, being satisfying without being too demanding.

The Guardian has an interesting, although sometimes complex, crossword often containing up-to-the-minute allusions and consistently featuring extensive cross-referencing between clues. The compilers are named, by pseudonyms, so after a while, solving for example an Araucaria can be like renewing an acquaintance with an old friend. The practical advantage of a system of named compilers is that you can frequently anticipate when a puzzle is going to be easy or difficult.

The Independent features a challenging crossword which is in style, content and general level of difficulty similar to *The Times*. The allusions and references in *The Independent* crossword are frequently bolder and more contemporary than those in *The Times* crossword, perhaps reflecting the younger profile of the paper's readership.

The *Telegraph* crossword, though not as challenging as those in *The Guardian*, *The Independent*, or *The Times*, is always enjoyable and is particularly good for building up a knowledge of the abbreviations, symbols and syntax needed to solve structural clues. The clues are in many ways more accessible to the novice solver, and it is therefore recommended as an excellent precursor to more advanced solving.

This brings us to the crossword that most adherents see as the ultimate daily challenge, *The Times*. Although the most difficult, this puzzle is not really the sole province of the elite, as it is seen by most people who do not tackle crosswords. It is closely monitored and edited for difficulty, neither the clues nor the answers requiring more than the occasional reference to a good desk dictionary. What makes *The Times* stand out is the consistently high quality of syntax and originality in the clues. It is rare that even on a Monday (usually the easiest day) there are not at least one or two that bring a quiet glow of inner satisfaction when solved.

Part of the reputation of *The Times* in recent years rests on the fact that it runs an annual National Crossword Championship, which has become extremely popular among solvers of all ages everywhere. For many years the undefeated champion was Dr John Sykes, the Oxford University Press lexicographer. Dr Sykes was famous for his accuracy and unsurpassed breadth of knowledge in solving crosswords, rather than for his pure speed. One of the most famous speed solvers of bygone days, apparently, was the Provost of Eton, who was reputed to be able to solve *The Times* crossword while boiling his breakfast egg. It used to be said that he liked his crosswords hard but not his egg!

Apart from *The Times* Championship, most national papers run a prize crossword on Saturdays. Unlike the Championship, these crosswords do not involve a trial against the clock, and though the puzzles are usually a little tougher than those appearing on weekdays, they are great fun to solve and send in — even if the chances of winning are not exactly guaranteed! Michael Mates, the Conservative MP, once held a party in the House of Commons to celebrate having won his first *Times* crossword competition after sending in completed puzzles for almost twenty years.

No doubt Mr Mates enjoyed solving every one of those prize puzzles plus all the other crosswords that he has almost certainly attempted and completed during those years. Whether you are tackling the *Mail* or *Express* (both of which have very enjoyable cryptics) or the real mindbenders in the weekend colour supplements (after you've disposed of the ones in the main papers, of course), you will be one of a growing number who have discovered the joys of the cryptic crosswords — a truly stimulating and rewarding intellectual pastime, and yours for the price of a paper.

Crosswords 1 – 10

The first ten puzzles are reasonably easy. The clues are representative of the sort of standard you might find in a cryptic such as the *Daily Mail*, *Daily Express* or occasionally in the *Daily Telegraph*. The clues do not contain any particularly obscure terms and the solutions should not require the use of a dictionary. There is a progression of difficulty from one puzzle to the next which has been established through averaging out the time taken to solve each one by a number of solvers of varying levels of experience.

The first ten puzzles contain against each clue a square-bracketed indication of the type of device being used. This is keyed to the explanations in the section **Cryptic Clue Types and Devices**, a summary of which is also available at the back of the book for ease of reference. By and large, the order of listing of the indications is designed to give an idea of the way the elements in each clue build up to form the solution. However, the indications are intended to function as a helpful pointer to the *type* of clue being looked at, rather than as an exhaustive dissection of every single element in the clue. Thus, for instance, where a clue contains more than one abbreviation, there is not an individual annotation for each abbreviation (except in a few more complex examples) as this would have looked cumbersome and could have become confusing. Neither have we indicated every instance of misleading punctuation, preferring to highlight those that seemed especially deceptive, or which caused our novice solvers particular problems.

As a further aid to beginners, we have also highlighted the definitional element of the clues (single definitions and quotation-based clues excepted for obvious reasons) in **bold** type. This is to allow solvers to concentrate on how the various devices work — which is particularly important in the early stages of learning how to do cryptic crosswords. In the case of double or multiple definition clues, we have tried to highlight the literal or least misleading information.

Finally, we have provided a head start in these early puzzles by filling in some of the solutions on the grids. The clues chosen for completion were selected either as being of more than usual difficulty or as being structurally helpful for solving and checking other tougher clues on the grid.

When solving the puzzles, remember that the **Two-way Crossword Glossary** contains a lot of useful information and that the **Help for Graded Puzzles** section explains many of the solutions in detail.

CROSSWORD NO. 1

ACROSS

4 Second coach **used to make tea** (8) [o,d]
8 **Cutlery** awarded as second prize? (6) [a]
9 **Come into view again** to cut down fruit (8) [d]
10 Period of time following brief **deficit** (8) [d]
11 **Delay** a robbery (4-2) [a]
12 Faulty machine requiring call initially to **person who will fix it** (8) [cii,nii]
13 Survival from past drinking bout? (8) [b]
16 **Confrontation** after demonstration is defeated (8) [d]
19 If you go to these, you may have gone too far (8) [b]
21 **Believe** favourable reputation (6) [a]
23 Perhaps the function of 1? (8) [b,r]
24 Nice oils could be used to make this **kind of polish** (8) [ci]
25 Embittered, Ralph keeps back **stock** (6) [h,g]
26 **Dotage** saw knees trembling (8) [ci]

DOWN

1 Boat is **not so heavy** (6) [a]
2 **Ruin** chance of extra run (9) [a]
3 Invest in the cloth? (6) [b]
4 Have a bit of exercise and become taller? (7,4,4) [b]
5 **Managing to touch** everyone separately in circle (8) [e]
6 **Instigate** politician being ensnared by awful lie (5) [o,e,cii]
7 **Rubbing out** is certain following initial error by artist (7) [d,nii,o]
14 Present conservative **collection** (9) [d,o]
15 Zip across the Atlantic from UK (8) [b]
17 **Brave woman** taking drug cure finally (7) [d,nii]
18 Lacking direction, **wander** with me instead! (7) [l,u]
20 Got up with bad leg attached to **kind of fastener** (6) [g,d,ci]
22 **Swallow**tails from Hyderabad, Kashmir, Delhi, Rangoon and Bangkok (5) [pii,ni]

CROSSWORD NO. 1

CROSSWORD NO. 2

ACROSS

1 It's amusing **having people for a meal** (12) [a]
9 **Exaggerate** concerning condition (9) [d]
10 **Sluggish** trainer tries taking part (5) [h]
11 **Design** fashionable camping equipment (6) [d]
12 Tree attendant is **civic dignitary** (8) [d]
13 Initially galloping about **field** (6) [nii,d]
15 **Designated** as indicated (8) [d]
18 Trick to attract **scorn** (8) [d]
19 **Church seats** completely straddled by holy men (6) [e,o]
21 Silent signal for **training equipment** (4-4) [d]
23 A tissue, we hear, might be appropriate for this **sudden attack**! (6) [i]
26 Heather, love, **this language is not understood** (5) [d,o]
27 **The head of a council** is a person initially dwelling in a place for some time (9) [nii,d]
28 **Someone trying to be like another** man, so I report in a confused way (12) [ci]

DOWN

1 **Wearing** rig done with style (7) [ci]
2 **Pay for someone** to negotiate (5) [a]
3 An ace tenor's wild at missing **sympathetic vibration** (9) [ciii,pi]
4 A girl heard **an expression of grief** (4) [i,d]
5 Irritates skinhead – it's **unnecessary** (8) [d,nii,pii]
6 **Din** from piano is excruciating (5) [h]
7 End **part of plug**? (8) [a]
8 Newspaperman following point-to-point is **very drunk** (6) [o,o,d]
14 **Decorate** in gold title on books (8) [d,o]
16 **Aim** for eleven to one on (9) [r,o,d]
17 **A dessert** order that is perfect (5-3) [a]
18 **Pamper** learned religious person embraced by old king (6) [q,e,o,piii]
20 Lieutenant protected by steep **cover** (7) [e,o]
22 **Brush** bedroom when little Edward has left (5) [f,o]
24 **Choose** from selection (5) [h]
25 Immerses every other one in **confusion** (4) [m]

CROSSWORD NO. 2

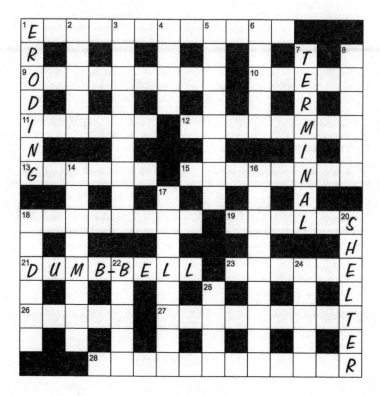

CROSSWORD NO. 3

ACROSS

1 Russian vehicle **not far from Middlesbrough** (6) [d]
4 Keeps company with royalty? (8) [b]
9 Bit of magic performed on deck? (4;5) [b]
11 Merle's fancy **man** (5) [ci]
12 Is he a farmer holding a **harvest bundle**? (5) [h]
13 Sounds like selling the **joy of cycling!** (9) [i]
15 **Born** in need (3) [h]
17 **Puzzling diversion** using lights (9) [b]
20 **Frightened** to make a mistake if in raging tide (9) [e,cii]
21 Desert **animal** (3) [a]
23 Verse points to **Chinese dialect** (9) [d,o]
25 Strange graduate **dance** (5) [d,o]
27 Some mechanised **plant** (5) [h]
28 Draw on garbled rot included in **preface** (9) [e,cii]
29 Terns go South in error with **another bird** (8) [cii,o]
30 Girl on board **fishes** (6) [e,o]

DOWN

1 Doubtless unsuitable as a lullaby! (4,4) [b]
2 Hymn for one who is late? (5) [b]
3 **Craftsman** with a terrific innovation (9) [ci]
5 All right round a **wood** (3) [o,e]
6 **Period** of enchantment (5) [a]
7 Sell off cheaply **what's left** (9) [a]
8 **Signals indifference** to second-hand carpets (6) [o,d]
10 **To make it up on the spot** is better all round (9) [e]
14 **Protester** I'd held in disagreement (9) [e,pi]
16 **Stretching** from stress (9) [d]
18 Does the salesman open this under strict instruction? (5,4) [b]
19 Flags out of river **boats** (8) [f,o]
22 **What pets may be given** to fight sickness initially (6) [d,nii]
24 Gangs of witches caught leaving **heated chambers** (5) [j]
26 **Climb upon** poetic steed (5) [a]
28 Intermittently filches **diamonds** (3) [m]

CROSSWORD NO. 3

CROSSWORD NO. 4

ACROSS

1 Security-conscious astronomer? (5,8) [b]
10 Nat is to be awkward and **stubborn** (9) [ci]
11 **Great annoyance** when old car doesn't start (5) [j]
12 Fool ultimately silly **fielder** (5) [d,nii]
13 **Laziness** at new church about grief (9) [d,o,o,e]
14 **Time** for making uniform? (7) [a]
16 'This blessed plot, this earth, this realm, this —' (*Richard II*) (7) [q]
18 **Soaking** bad twinge? About time! (7) [ci,e,o,p]
20 To match **completely** (7) [d]
21 **Elevate** damaged automobiles without wheels (9) [cii,j]
23 Sounds like a way to get **heavenly food** (5) [i]
24 **Accurate** former deed (5) [d]
25 A tragic member resolved to be **practical** (9) [cii,o]
26 **Patronizing** criminal going down (13) [d]

DOWN

2 **Bankrupt** rude about advocate's third letter (9) [e,nii]
3 Bald men aren't this **dangerous** (5) [a]
4 **Displaying** organ in part of building (7) [e]
5 Altered cycling **pedal** (7) [ci]
6 Car fixture might be a bright idea for miners (9) [b]
7 **Gas** container is near gondola (5) [h]
8 Perhaps Latvian tormentor? **It's hard to say** (6,7) [d]
9 Game played on Tongan island? (8,5) [b]
15 **Began** to instruct leading driver (9) [d,nii]
17 Head of English town off **somewhere in North Virginia** (9) [j]
19 Manx cat after lightweight **overblown swimmer** (7) [pii,j,d]
20 No right to generate changes **between twelve and twenty** (7) [j,cii]
22 British eggs sent up **well done** (5) [o,g,d]
23 Took part in a play where actions speak louder than words (5) [b]

CROSSWORD NO. 4

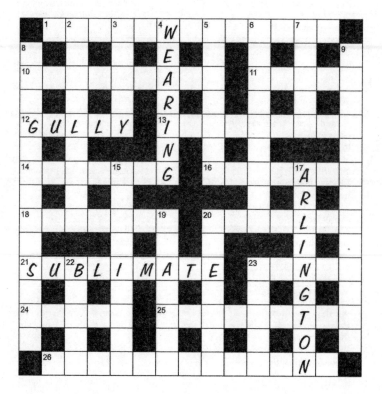

CROSSWORD NO. 5

ACROSS

1 **Shrewd** like pupil kicking ecstasy (6) [d,j,o]
4 River **plant** (6) [a]
9 **Maple** in cultivated acre (4) [ci]
10 **Eminence** of Conservative following concert in progress (10) [o,d]
11 A doctor overwhelmed by disapproval for **grass** (6) [e,o]
12 Fairly often combined with this, paradoxically, when roundly beaten (8) [b]
13 With 'shining morning face', Shakespeare's crept 'like snail unwillingly' (9) [q]
15 **Drama** children may enjoy (4) [a]
16 **Lots** of post redistributed (4) [ci]
17 A lame bird's recovery is **highly appreciated** (9) [ci]
21 Note Queen Elizabeth I twice contracting **tropical disease** (8) [o,d,o]
22 **Fail** to work on the farm (6) [a]
24 CIA suppressing fictitious Rendell **heroine** (10) [e,ci,piii]
25 Initially night owls often nap at this **time of day** (4) [ni]
26 Fellow reportedly sincere enough for Wilde? (6) [a,i]
27 Master arranged **division of pupils according to ability** (6) [ci]

DOWN

1 Could one really describe Noah's vessel as this **old-fashioned**? (7) [b,i]
2 **Soundly beat** some towpath robbers (5) [h]
3 Oil spot ruined **surface material** (7) [ci]
5 Visit **to consult a reference book** (4,2) [a]
6 **Hairy swimmer** responsible for a fleet war breaking out (5-4) [ci]
7 Rugby Union meeting **out of town** (7) [o,d]
8 **Famous beauty spot** in Beds with ancient uplands (8,5) [o,pi,piii,d]
14 **Beaten** duke routed in disorder (9) [o,cii]
16 **Proposition** before young lady is announced (7) [d,i]
18 Lifted motorway machinery for **operation** (7) [g,o,d]
19 **Space to stretch out** for the French husband? (7) [d]
20 The art shop stocks **red cards** (6) [h]
23 Lightweight **cat**? (5) [pii,a]

CROSSWORD NO. 5

CROSSWORD NO. 6

ACROSS

1 **Old** type of novel (10) [a]
8 **Ascetic** bear! (4) [a]
10 Brown possibly describes Greenham or Wandsworth, for instance (6,4) [a]
11 **Stream** of headless fish (4) [j]
13 Reveals mystery to **a few** (7) [ci]
15 Hush rude sound! It's **acute** (6) [d,i]
16 Gunner's head becoming right **coward** (6) [l]
17 **Leading lady** in grave need made East Australian mad (4,4,7) [cii,o]
18 Prepare food that is **eaten by many Americans** (6) [d,o]
20 **Crooked** swing, loosely dropping head down (6) [pi,k]
21 Directions to police **to prosecute** (7) [o,d]
22 One infiltrating back-tracking union produces **collapse** (4) [o,g,e]
25 Dim intuition without it could be **lessening** (10) [ciii]
26 **Situation** in which Shiite throws out greeting (4) [j]
27 Does signing on here imply queuing for extended periods? (6,4) [b]

DOWN

2 **Indian** from Brahmin caste (4) [h]
3 Herb, we hear, in **season** (4) [i]
4 Uphill detour, with roundabout replacing turn, is **firmly established** (6) [g,l]
5 **Greenkeeper?** (15) [b,pii]
6 Lying upon my back and resting first sections **of the lower spine** (6) [ni]
7 **Constant companion** of Miss China (10) [d,piii]
9 Team up with football club starting **in an easterly direction** (10) [d]
12 Doctor in Troon is tense **wind player** (10) [o,e,d,nii]
13 Affectionate reference to a child **may be humbug!** (7) [a]
14 **Plant** that can be found in Switzerland (7) [a]
15 Mussolini in a state, engulfed by emotional pressure from **femme fatale** (10) [q,cii,e]
19 Sinned in an idiomatically colourful way? (6) [b]
20 **Charge** account application (6) [o,d]
23 Might this philosopher be turning in his grave? (4) [b]
24 Can one discover herein a **prolific poet**? (4) [h,u]

CROSSWORD NO. 6

CROSSWORD NO. 7

ACROSS

1 Fool one in company with **Shakespeare's Lieutenant** (6) [o,e,o,q]

5 **Stirred** by tower in part of India (8) [e,nii]

9 All clues read over so that I can begin each **puzzle** (8) [ni]

10 **Unpleasant smell** from roast enchilada (6) [h]

11 Farm plot ploughed up to make **raised area** (8) [ci]

12 In church, journalist **moved imperceptibly** (6) [d,o]

13 Typical state of America? (8) [b]

15 Composer from the Arctic Circle? (4) [b]

17 Get out **basin** (4) [a]

19 **As counselling** avoids tangled lines of communication (8) [ci,d,o]

20 **Achieve balance** by redirecting squats (6) [l]

21 Firmness proverbially associated with soft touch (4,4) [b,q]

22 **Colourful expressions** of fools with money for trifles initially (6) [l,o,ni]

23 **She** is a beauty! (8) [d]

24 Late pilot of **a Tiger Moth, perhaps** (5,3) [d,piii]

25 Uninitiated unruly children make **mistakes** (6) [j]

DOWN

2 **Praise** a revolting peasant surrounding a pass (8) [e,q]

3 **Generous** with wine in shop (8) [e]

4 Wild duck, as detour, **flew much higher** (9) [pi,o,cii]

5 A mismatch is **grounds for divorce** (15) [a]

6 **Effectiveness** of drug measure on Cyprus (7) [d,o]

7 **Mexican cowboy** raced and caught Superman (8) [o,d]

8 **Two-faced** die-hard left in disarray (8) [cii,o]

14 Cool cheat managed **a kind of bar**? (9) [ci]

15 No resistance to Brian accepting mobile home in which he might live (8) [j,e,ci,u]

16 Call up rising inspiration in **beginning again** (8) [e,g]

17 **Unwilling recruit thus led** to be hearty convert (2,3,3) [ci]

18 Argumentative **student**? (8) [b]

19 **Try** to seduce (7) [d]

CROSSWORD NO. 7

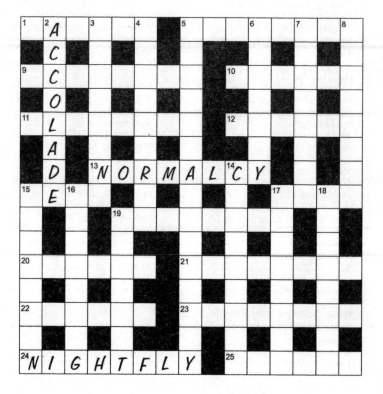

CROSSWORD NO. 8

ACROSS

1 **Funny** mineral found in mountain pass (7) [e]
5 Coleman's initial substitution for first ingredient of mustard **sauce** (7) [l]
9 Central aim of a lord's ball? (6,5) [b,piii]
10 Imperial heavyweight (3) [b,pii]
11 **Father's** an aged chap (3,3) [a]
13 **Highlights importance** of bearings outside lock (8) [e,o]
15 **Ambassador** of outstanding quality (10) [a]
16 Is it permissible to parcel last of auction **lots**? (4) [e,nii]
18 Fly-by-night? (4) [b,pi]
19 Dashes over deserted heather **on horseback** (10) [d,g,o]
22 **Churchman** lancing a boil! (8) [ci]
23 **One who is promised** public money is one note short (6) [f]
25 **Strange phenomenon** first of all under frequent observation (3) [ni]
26 Forecasts **possibilities** (11) [a]
28 Sender confused about title of **final recipient** (3-4) [ci,e,o]
29 Really unknown quantity included **in reference system** (7) [o,e]

DOWN

1 Mozart, for example, has no right **to write music** (7) [j]
2 **Soft earth** in Bermuda (3) [h]
3 Copper fit to hold record for **being guilty** (8) [o,e,o]
4 **Hear** old pianist (4) [i,s,u]
5 Accurate directions for cooking **lobster or shrimp** (10) [cii,o]
6 Rustles up, perhaps, a bit of **a late evening snack** (6) [h]
7 **Bearing witness** at trial by leaderless state (11) [d,j]
8 **Tudor** soap, perhaps! (7) [a]
12 Where people used to go under for punishment? (7,4) [b]
14 Engineers coach **someone who holds back** (10) [o,d]
17 Swimming dace tiddlers – 50% **hooked** (8) [cii,j]
18 **Such an article** may be a cheek (7) [a,pii]
20 Greek relieved to be **bribed** (7) [o,d]
21 **Butcher's wares** supply modern woman with nice stew (6) [e,ci]
24 Each one is **a fairy** (4) [d,o]
27 **King's** dog's name (3) [a]

CROSSWORD NO. 8

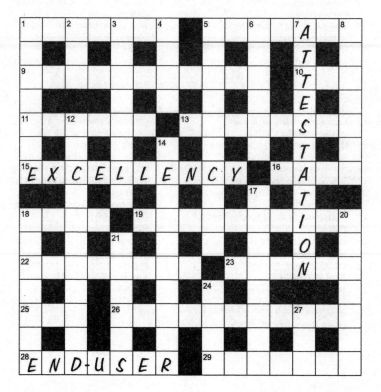

CROSSWORD NO. 9

ACROSS

1 **Settles** advance payment with teams (8) [d]
5 Paul's first steps taken here? At least in part (6) [b]
10 **Honest** direction (15) [a]
11 **Extortionist** stealing a line from one who once trod the boards (7) [a,j,o]
12 Danger troubled Eastern **magnate** (7) [cii,o]
13 Back in Baghdad, no canard exposes **crawler** (8) [h,g]
15 **Complete** setback without army reserves (5) [u,g,o,e]
17 **Business** custom (5) [a]
19 Spilt acid near **bright light** (8) [ci]
22 Property displayed by those who 7 (7) [b,r]
23 **Witty remark** made during Tripos term (7) [h]
24 Mechanical study of current interest, no doubt (15) [b]
25 On which to sit as you prepare to drive off? (6) [b]
26 **Small, fleet** vessels (8) [a,pi]

DOWN

1 None spoke of this **close relative** (6) [i]
2 Where to get the lowdown on cheap offers? (7,8) [b]
3 **Silly** fool in charge (7) [d,o]
4 There is turbulent **air up above** (5) [ci]
6 **Fully briefed,** sailor takes a breather outside (7) [o,d,e]
7 Endure punishment to the point where **you cannot move** (5,5,5) [d]
8 Duly send letters, sorted **hastily** (8) [ci]
9 **Not watching** unusual stance of one who's in? (3,5) [a]
14 **Teller** rushed over to desert with gold (8) [g,d]
16 Players with whom managers may disagree? (8) [b]
18 Knotted tie lent **style** (6) [ci]
20 The end of the road for Cleopatra? (7) [b]
21 Home of tailless cat? (6) [pii,b]
23 Two boys **belonging to Her Majesty**? (5) [d]

CROSSWORD NO. 9

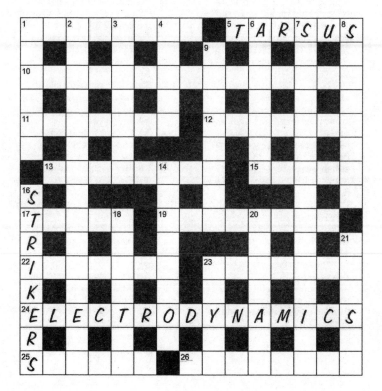

CROSSWORD NO. 10

ACROSS

1 Runs into fish in **drain** (6) [e,o]
4 Is old journal **suitable material to draw on**? (3,5) [d,s]
10 Weather malevolent? Take out **this type of underwear** (7) [h]
11 Girl has spoken **of local chief** (7) [d]
12 One no good initially again tries **practising** (10) [d,o,ni]
13 Sort out sink **for use on 4**? (4) [ci,r]
15 Suspend boxer possibly **looking cowed** (7) [d]
17 Picture set for **field event** (4-3) [d]
19 Problem originating at the back **part of horse's leg** (7) [nii,d]
21 Roam with pie about **these shops** (7) [ci]
23 **Hit** a seedy kind of joint (4) [a]
24 Immediately reformed queues, being **dignified** (10) [d,o,ci]
27 Note little fellow from No 10 is **negligible** (7) [d,r,h]
28 Knot attaches **men's fashion accessories** (7) [d]
29 Any chits rewritten for **old countryman?** (8) [ci,pii]
30 Reptiles of a calculating nature? (6) [b]

DOWN

1 Teachers' joint **post** (9) [d]
2 **Butler's paradise** paradoxically nowhere (7) [q,ci]
3 **Seize** and recommend a demolition (10) [ci]
5 **Recollect** nice rimes (9) [u,ci]
6 **Yields** tars (4) [a]
7 Score then cut **vegetable** (7) [d]
8 **Registers** expensive car (5) [a]
9 See lakes evenly stocked with **wildlife** (4) [m]
14 Take in **embrace** (10) [a]
16 Italian for example abandoned **most sensitive areas!** (9) [ci]
18 **Passes over** stanza in Arts form (9) [e,ci]
20 Spruce, poplar, ironwood, nutmeg, nicotinia, elder, yew: all originally **here**? (7) [ni]
22 Religious Education old choir **need** (7) [o,s,d]
23 **Searches** for companies accepting medical graduate (5) [o,e]
25 Artists' sugar-daddy? (4) [b]
26 Martha maybe partly raised by **wet-nurse?** (4) [h,g]

CROSSWORD NO. 10

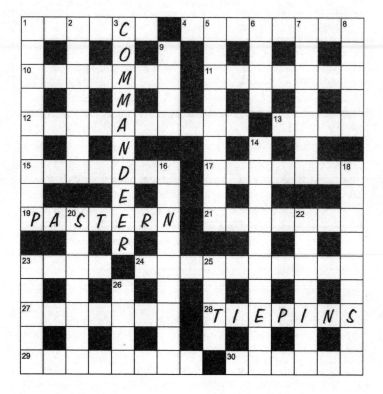

A Short History of the Crossword

The tradition of acrostics and word-play stretches right back to Greek and Roman times: Cicero, for instance, records how the sibyls used riddles to prophesy the future, and there are various well-documented examples of how early Christians employed enigmatic devices to reveal their message to other believers.

Yet it was not until the Victorian age that wordgames started to gain ground as a form of popular entertainment, with the appearance of numerous books of puzzles and brain-teasers. Inventive though they were, however, the Victorians never really progressed beyond a simple form of puzzle based on the word square, a group of words arranged to read the same both horizontally and vertically.

In fact, it was the Americans who took things a stage further. On 21 December 1913, the first genuine crossword to be published in a newspaper appeared among a number of more conventional puzzles in the Sunday *Fun* supplement of the *New York World*. Called a 'Word Cross', it consisted of a diamond-shaped grid with definitional clues to the intersecting solutions and was compiled by Arthur Wynne, an immigrant from Liverpool. This type of puzzle proved so popular that by 1923 most American newspapers had a crossword; by this time, the craze had started to spread to Britain, where it quickly became accepted as a national pastime.

The first regular crossword in the UK was published by the *Sunday Express* in 1924, while puzzles started appearing in the *Daily Telegraph* a year later. *The Times* lays claim to being the first British paper to have a crossword appearing on a daily basis (1 February 1930) — although there is some dispute about this.

These early crosswords had essentially straightforward definitional clues with barely a hint of cryptic in them. Indeed, American puzzles remained definitional until recently — even though some of the clues and solutions were highly obscure. British crosswords, on the other hand, gradually started to move away from the established, literal type of clue some time ago. Devices such as anagrams (simply labelled 'anagram' at first), double definitions, obscure indications and all the other misleading strategies are now a commonplace part of the cryptic crossword as we know it today.

The conventions that govern the shape of the diagram, and the rules of fair play in setting clues, developed largely through a process of evolution — much like the English constitution. Attempts have been made by famous setters such as Afrit and Ximenes to frame rules for writing crossword clues: much currently received wisdom is based on their work. For those who are interested in studying the subject of clueing, Don Manley's *Chambers Crossword Manual* provides an entertaining and accessible introduction.

Crosswords 11 – 20

This section starts off with puzzles of about the same standard as the first ten, gradually increasing in difficulty. The more difficult puzzles towards the end are of a standard roughly on a par with an easy-to-average puzzle in one of the broadsheet dailies. Once again, neither the clues nor the solutions contain any words that should require the use of a dictionary.

In these crosswords, however, we have not highlighted the definitional element of the clues: you will have to go through the puzzles and sort this out for yourself. Neither are there any partially completed grids.

What you do still get are the indications of clue devices bracketed after each clue. (You should by now be fairly familiar with the alphabetical labelling used for the more common devices.) This and the **Two-way Crossword Glossary** should enable you to tackle most of the clues in these puzzles without too much difficulty. Once again, if you do have problems with a particular clue, consult the **Help for Graded Puzzles** section.

CROSSWORD NO. 11

ACROSS

1 Full of beans after drinking this? (6) [b]
4 & 2 *Dn* Ship's Officer goes to Welsh town to find chatty bird (7,5) [d,q]
9 Head's golden rule, we're told (9) [i]
10 Pole ultimately forms axe-handle (5) [nii,d]
11 Bury together (5) [a]
12 'And smooth as monumental —' (*Othello*) (9) [q]
13 Atone for resistance from former corsair (7) [o,d,f]
15 Dress worn over one's behind (6) [d,g,nii]
17 Purpose in putting energy into explosive (6) [d,o,e]
19 Beg to replant a National Trust tree (7) [cii,o]
22 Furnish books catering for future needs (9) [d,o]
24 Resistance unit stumbled through ack-ack on this beach (5) [cii,o]
26 Sound from soprano is exquisite (5) [h]
27 Take choir about Jerusalem, for example (9) [ci]
28 Grid used outside for training climbers (7) [b]
29 Lost smoker's accessory's not hot (6) [j,o]

DOWN

1 Whim of island church (7) [d,o]
2 See 4 *Ac* (5)
3 Tear a strip off former chief officer with irate outburst (9) [o,d,ci]
4 Late Passover get-together (7) [d,pi,pii]
5 Dad's gratitude, of course (5) [d]
6 Girl, with exercise, fit for anything! (9) [d,o,u]
7 He wrote not a line (6) [d,o]
8 Work I took in for narcotic (6) [o,d]
14 Peter to act silently in this Christmas show? (9) [q,d]
16 Behaves in a backward-looking manner and withdraws keeping nothing (9) [e,o]
18 Created space to protect one's pedal extremities (7) [ci,u]
19 Object denoted entirety (6) [f]
20 Score boxes to chase ornamentation (7) [e]
21 Pest in reconstructed instrument (6) [ci]
23 Immaculate conception? (5) [a]
25 Othello, possibly reported French lover (5) [i]

CROSSWORD NO. 11

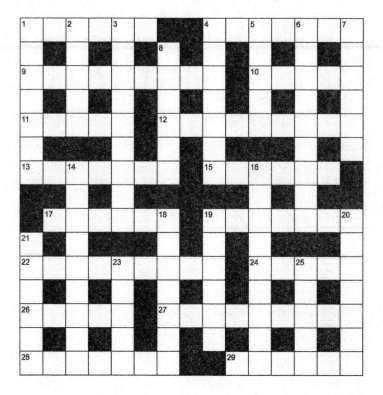

CROSSWORD NO. 12

ACROSS

1 You need these, we hear, to see small particles (6) [i]
5 Vehicle following taxi over to casino game (8) [d,g]
9 Girl Scout leader occasionally seen after dark (5,3) [a]
10 Piece of metal is sometimes very flexible (6) [h]
11 Preoccupied with eye, by the sound of it (8) [b,i]
12 Guide's often instructed thus to corrupt (4,2) [a]
13 Frenchman in grenade explosion finds policeman (8) [o,cii]
15 Goddess leads a double life apparently (4) [d]
17 Detailed lavish addition (4) [j]
19 Travelling salesman upset by pain runs for minister (8) [cii,d,o]
20 Measure device to use (6) [nii,d]
21 13, for example, creates a pure one (8) [r,ci]
22 Many attending Ravel symphony give cause for amazement (6) [o,cii]
23 Most can't vote before reaching this age (8) [a]
24 True saint out East who can be barely discerned (8) [cii,j,o]
25 Lying low to avoid this punishment, perhaps (6) [a]

DOWN

2 Models rearrange a rap song (8) [ci]
3 Enclosures for animals eating heather (8) [pi,e]
4 Powdered steer horn used to make pastry (9) [ci]
5 Protection for despatch rider on Russian front? (9,6) [b]
6 Boxer, perhaps, since he reformed (7) [q,ci]
7 What's left long after a declaration of independence is, with hesitation, overturned (8) [d,o,g]
8 Hardy heroine about to approve meek nature (8) [q,e]
14 Graduate going to express suspicion to Indian landlord finds his boss (9) [o,d]
15 One who went into print on an engagement? (8) [b]
16 Fashionable drink lacking body? (2,6) [d]
17 Set edition of red paper (8) [ci]
18 Ten fauns gambolling free (8) [ci]
19 One in support of leader (7) [e]

CROSSWORD NO. 12

CROSSWORD NO. 13

ACROSS

1 Perhaps a single log (6) [a]
4 After dinner request for entry permit (8) [a]
10 Royal mistress with an early form of beehive! (9) [b,q]
11 Fantasy about mother's boxing (5) [e]
12 Perhaps kid soldier needs to make private escape (8) [d]
13 Instruction to loquacious luggage handler? (4,2) [b]
15 The aching part everyone separately considered (4) [h]
17 Put in grave appearance for formal meeting (9) [d]
20 Asia, for example, is temperate (9) [a]
21 What seer discerned partly from entrails (4) [h]
24 Conveyed after a second compliance (6) [o,d]
25 Condense company papers containing Maxwell's initial (8) [o,e,nii]
28 Region round the centre of Genoa is part of an ancient amphitheatre (5) [e,nii]
29 Revived battered cedar tree (9) [ci]
30 Cure for love-sickness, perhaps (8) [b]
31 A churchman started to become confused (6) [d,o,d]

DOWN

1 Substituted parcel Ed repackaged (8) [ci]
2 Reach tiptop heavenly body (5) [d,nii]
3 Actually about League member (6) [o,d]
5 Light-hearted tune has funny ending (4) [d,ni]
6 Stupidly deviates from bedtime prescription (8) [ci]
7 Finished with old headgear after flood (9) [d,o,s]
8 Plant used to split atom (6) [d,ci]
9 Part of the hole, so to speak (9) [b,i]
14 Strengthen control for the Church (9) [d,o]
16 High-flier's point of view (5,4) [b]
18 Upright Pole used to fly the flag (8) [piii,b]
19 Biased description of deficient 1 *Ac*, perhaps (3,5) [a,r]
22 Best start pineapple without second fruit (6) [nii,d,j]
23 Sort of paste to be avoided in middle age, if possible (6) [a]
26 Praise for former charge, we hear (5) [d,i]
27 Support the tiresome child (4) [d,o]

CROSSWORD NO. 13

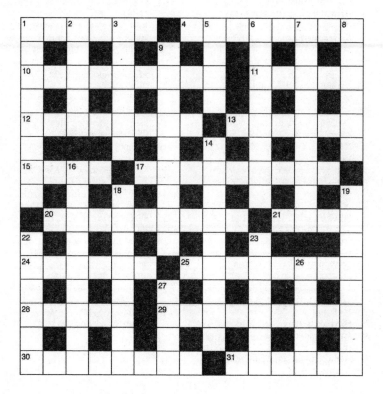

CROSSWORD NO. 14

ACROSS

1 Who knows? This type of question remains unanswered (10) [b]
8 Block return of large sums of money (4) [g]
10 Tacky American game? (5,5) [b]
11 Somewhere to store a variety of paints perhaps (4) [cii]
13 Cast light on information about file (7) [e]
15 Going upstairs (6) [a,pii]
16 Musical movements in overtures from Rossini, Offenbach, Nielsen, Debussy, Orff and Schoenberg (6) [ni]
17 Crazy interpretation of a dream has intrinsically a kind of charm (3,2,1,5,4) [ci,d,e,ci]
18 Open display (6) [a]
20 Awkward refusal to race in Kentucky (6) [d,o,e,o]
21 Paying organization to keep quiet in Barking (7) [ci,e,o,piii]
22 Standard article from Roman constitution (4) [cii,j]
25 Tackle inside of cold faulty boiler, which may be put right (10) [e,o,d,ci,u]
26 Say a mantra backwards? That's too much for an Indian tongue (4) [h,g]
27 Of the sinner reformed, the saint is this! (10) [ci,u]

DOWN

2 Barely tolerate mediocre journalist (4) [a]
3 Advice about right holiday (4) [o,e]
4 What could come about from the disintegration of Ulster (6) [ci]
5 Present day vision? (9,6) [b]
6 Minor points separating two sides (6) [o,e,o]
7 Truly hopes to order chair covering (10) [ci]
9 Liberals once described a policy for the motorist (5,10) [a]
12 Hungry flier fed by prior arrangement (4,2,4) [ci]
13 Faint appearance of 5 in Dickens story? (7) [a,q,r]
14 Lack of significance Macbeth accorded to biography (7) [a,q]
15 Well-known figure at Lloyds? (6,4) [b]
19 Plane that flew both north and south here in the States (6) [a,piii]
20 Thing assembled to support King's champion (6) [cii,o,u]
23 Authorized Napoleon's island retreats (4) [g]
24 Half man, half beast, this creature is still single! (4) [d,o]

CROSSWORD NO. 14

CROSSWORD NO. 15

ACROSS

1 Acting royally? (10) [b,q]
6 Large chunk of material from physics laboratory (4) [h]
10 Seafood starters often can taste of pretty unpalatable stuff (7) [ni]
11 Clergyman who searched every crook and nanny! (7) [b,q]
12 Craft for river trips out East (9) [d,cii,o]
13 Barnaby taking girl's head in rough embrace (5) [q,nii,e]
14 *La Mer* translated for this country (5) [ci]
15 Breaking fasts, I die to be fully fed (9) [ci]
17 Lorded over and loved to embrace bird (9) [e]
20 This animal, by right, could be a stinker! (5) [j]
21 Heard by, for example, one playing bit part (5) [i,a]
23 Type of fever a lad suffers with right lung (9) [cii,o]
25 Nasty stain resulting from upsetting Indian, perhaps (3,4) [b]
26 Beat chap for touching line (7) [d]
27 Ringing this before dinner could make George cross, perhaps (4) [a,piii]
28 Champion's exploit in a French action (10) [d,e]

DOWN

1 Examine soft dress (5) [o,d]
2 With unhappy net loss sadly contemplates medium term (9) [cii,j]
3 Former fairy psychically linked through trial and error (14) [d]
4 Sack infernal American waitress? (7) [a/b]
5 Emerging when finally on the way up (7) [nii,d]
7 Idle partner gets worried look? (5) [cii,o,u]
8 Length of cloth in exchange of goods for drinks supplier (9) [e]
9 Work concerned prose writing (14) [ci]
14 Changing colour may be a ruddy cheek (9) [b]
16 'Our meddling — Misshapes the beauteous forms of things' (Wordsworth) (9) [q]
18 Screw up directions after getting drunk? (7) [d,o]
19 Conscript finds raft in river (7) [e]
22 End of tie in intricate knot for remembrance (5) [ci,e,nii]
24 Trade uncommonly highly thought of (5) [ci]

CROSSWORD NO. 15

CROSSWORD NO. 16

ACROSS

1 Younger son preparing for commission (5) [a]
4 Grew less from ploughed acres? Indeed! (9) [ci,e,pii]
9 Poetic description of Snow White, perhaps (3,6) [b,piii]
10 Ron taking exercise? On the contrary, flat out (5) [e,o]
11 Join in token listening (6) [h]
12 Treaders worked with pointed teeth (8) [ci]
14, 16, 22 *Dn*, 29 *Ac*, 6 *Dn* Classic story of war told about early Italian group of states (7,3,4,2,3,5,6) [q,i,d]
16 See 14 (4)
19 Odes rewritten to a certain measure (4) [ci]
20 Wobble unsteadily about and note regular movement (3,3,4) [cii,e,o]
22 Oddly covers debts, having lost five hundred in ignominious fashion (8) [f,o,e]
23 Discover cause of noise (6) [a]
26 Characteristic of one in small Italian restaurant (5) [o,e]
27 Device levels stone (9) [d]
28 Concerned about back-tracking in tax demand initially (9) [o,cii,nii]
29 See 14 (5)

DOWN

1 With Italian nurse Edward struggled (9) [d,o]
2 Succeed in losing trainee post (5) [j]
3 Impale and paralyse (8) [a]
4 It's senseless to cull four hundred more (4) [l]
5 An extra two would add a further hundred years to this anniversary (10) [j,b]
6 See 14 (6)
7 Brief dip leaves something to be desired (9) [d]
8 Fear of the cadre a democracy entertains (5) [h]
13 Early botanists worked on their slabs (10) [ci]
15 Criticize one coming in players' entrance (9) [d,o,e,pi]
17 Teutonic sound coming from manger before its reconstruction (3,6) [d,cii]
18 Control often necessary in settlement of insurance claims (8) [a]
21 Brown in charge of the country (6) [d,o]
22 See 14 (3,2)
24 God, how stuck up! (2,3) [a]
25 Raised for food, we're told (4) [i]

CROSSWORD NO. 16

CROSSWORD NO. 17

ACROSS

1 Hired hand at the wheel? (9) [b]
6 The old way, right, is more discreet (5) [s,d,o]
9 *High Noon* hailed by the Irish? (3,2,3,7) [piii,b]
10 She also returns in comfort (6) [e,g]
11 Take off belt and repair accident damage (8) [a]
13 Tradesmen who may use auto-suggestion (3,7) [b]
14 Battled, we're told, for stronghold (4) [i]
16 Poor chap embracing sweetheart (4) [nii,e]
17 Removed thread from such tinted weaving (10) [ci]
19 Conservative Bar hesitate to find 6 *Ac* (8) [o,d,r]
20 Memorized and readily available? On the contrary one way and another (3,3) [a,g]
23 Young genius, investing company in highly valued issue (10,5) [e,o,d]
24 Try to experience flavour (5) [a]
25 Desecrated a green hill for a power source (9) [ci,d]

DOWN

1 Quotes sound views (5) [i]
2 Suitability of relevant point (15) [d,o]
3 Struggle with the stiff part of the match (5,3) [ci]
4 Sound comeback by leader of Halle appropriated by English Chamber Orchestra (4) [ni,o,e]
5 Enumerate initial requirements revised for pay (10) [cii,nii]
6 What airline pilots do to arouse feelings? (4,2) [a]
7 Extremely painful compass direction for rambler? (5,2,3,5) [b]
8 Remembered with sense of loss your last bird, Edward (9) [nii,d,o]
12 First of botanists down in heather floundering about (10) [nii,d,e]
13 Light relief for the funny bone? (5,4) [a]
15 What 1 *Ac* may do for officer's vehicle (5,3) [r,a]
18 Take out Bunter's form (6) [a,q]
21 Half-timbered royal house? (5) [b]
22 Scottish poet detailed stream in his vernacular (4) [j]

CROSSWORD NO. 17

CROSSWORD NO. 18

ACROSS

1 Members' commonly held discussion (6) [b,piii]
4 Crude SAS manoeuvre involving second-hand vehicles (4,4) [ci,b]
10 Wooster's farewell to broken old pipe (6,3) [d,ci]
11 Get a citizen's contribution understood (5) [h]
12 Drama follows one who adapted music case to carry a gun (7) [d,q]
13 Uneasy, it veers about (7) [ci,pi]
14 March past when this begins (5) [b]
15 Hardy people take hits back and forth (8) [g,d]
18 Thunderous sea unusual central element in his paintings? (8) [h]
20 Shock a quiet friend (5) [o,d]
23 Rig vote to produce a loss of balance (7) [ci]
25 Books suitable for bed? (7) [b]
26 Strange means of identification? (5) [ci]
27 Loquacious Senora Peron reflected on speech (9) [d,g]
28 Representative figures found in American house (8) [b,piii]
29 Popular sayings of present times (6) [o,d]

DOWN

1 European aeronaut noted by Wagner (8) [a,q]
2 Young chicken's right to be protected by old one (7) [o,e]
3 Sneaks revealed Archer's inside story (4,5) [q,piii,e]
5 Outstanding, of course, in a strange way (14) [d]
6 Fruit consumed in the outskirts of Damascus (5) [e,ni]
7 Man from 1 *Dn* leaving sale where price-cutting is guaranteed (7) [r,j,b]
8 Tester may be the one who compiles this (6) [ci]
9 For this commentator, in particular, cricket's about having a drink afterwards! (6,8) [d]
16 Prepare group for the militia (9) [d]
17 Sparkles, even when first tenor is demoted (8) [l]
19 Eight going to Crewe, we're told – but not by train! (7) [b,i]
21 What you might be doing when suffering right inside (7) [e,o]
22 First lady's not disheartened entering functions (6) [d,j]
24 Patch where badger may be found (5) [a,d]

CROSSWORD NO. 18

CROSSWORD NO. 19

ACROSS

1 Main cause of internal disorder (11) [b]
9 Barrie's darling dog (4) [piii,q]
10 Abbreviated solution that an 'S' could stand for? (5,6) [b,pi,pii,piii]
11 Loud blast heard from stereo equipment (2,2) [i]
14 Potentially successful idea for a first course (7) [a]
16 React explosively to partner in card game (6) [cii,o]
17 Red-coated soldier in custody (6) [e,pii]
18 An extra vestment for the priest (3) [d,o]
20 Mysteriously recasts Garbo, perhaps (7) [ci]
21 Frenzied love bites may ultimately lead to a weight problem! (7) [o,cii,nii]
22 One who was entitled to come in from the cold (3) [b,q]
24 Men are manipulated to change designation (6) [ci]
26 Georgia ate up acceptable cake (6) [o,d,ci,o]
27 Malicious gossip about conservative footwear (7) [o,e,pi]
28 Dissolute firm (4) [a]
31 Circus act performing nude, we are told (7,4) [d,i]
32 Lion family misses start of journey (4) [j]
33 Widespread feeling after Mafeking, no doubt! (5,6) [b,q]

DOWN

2 Reflective nymph? (4) [b]
3 Type of gold found in street (4) [e,o]
4 Virgin is hounded, by sound of it (6) [i]
5 Opening below the bridge (7) [b]
6 Sounds like bird could be done to a turn on this (6) [i]
7 Excellent scheme for making money perhaps (7,4) [b]
8 Maybe sat in sun abroad with a bored expression (3,2,3,3) [t,d,piii]
12 Former panel reassembled to produce changes in sentencing policy (5,6) [ci]
13 Striking team at the Oval, for instance (7,4) [b]
14 Mists shrouding river tributaries (7) [e,o]
15 Restoration novel has genuine binding (7) [e]
18 Animal in crevasse (3) [h]
19 Issue booty unevenly (3) [nii]
23 Chewing a pea can be a cure for all ills (7) [ci]
25 Claire, head over heels, is sweet (6) [k]
26 Ramshackle arrangement meant unhappily leaving store (6) [ciii]
29 Lovable girl beheaded victim (4) [j]
30 Open pub with key (4) [d,o]

CROSSWORD NO. 19

CROSSWORD NO. 20

ACROSS

1 Individual student accepted though not very bright (5) [e,o]
4 Charmed by oriental woman who is fascinating in bed (9) [o,d,e]
9 Victory won at this battle (9) [b]
10 Less bitter dog perhaps given an outing (5) [j]
11 Not in suitable uniform (6) [d]
12 Leave vehicle on road near Mayfair (4,4) [d,u]
14 Writers of playful material? (10) [b]
16 Retreating before this erupts! (4) [g]
19 Harps on about snag (4) [ci]
20 Fluid runs from this plant (10) [d]
22 Sole power game (8) [a]
23 A paper edited to do this daily (6) [ci]
26 Greene Man entitled to a bronze medal? (5) [piii,q,a]
27 Might publish principal concern (4,5) [d]
28 Citrus pith found in European country yields sweet aroma (9) [e]
29 Shot in the dark part of rogue's strategy (5) [h]

DOWN

1 New copper turned on Organization (9) [o,cii,piii]
2 Inclined to speak fast (5) [i]
3 Disastrous hairs growing from ear, about lobe initially (8) [d,o,nii]
4 Insects frequently annoying the programmer (4) [a]
5 Licence that is supported by partner's guarantees (10) [d,o]
6 Lines made by carts meandering round the middle of Carrickfergus (6) [ci,nii,e]
7 I'm present in honour of future state (9) [d] .
8 Odd, for example, to resort to subterfuge (5) [cii,o]
13 It's a wonder I can work and remain calm in a riot (7,3) [ci]
15 Plate banked mainly here in South America (9) [b]
17 Following shock, these make for a smooth ride (9) [u]
18 Exchanging partner somewhere in the East End (8) [d]
21 Spinner used to play snooker occasionally (6) [a]
22 Distinctive idea if combined with French word (5) [d]
24 Directions to girl to follow (5) [o,d]
25 German wine said to come from this (4) [u,i]

CROSSWORD NO. 20

Famous and Infamous Clues

In the previous feature on the history of the crossword, we mentioned the way in which the art of the crossword has gradually evolved over the years. Every so often, a clue will appear which is so original or so elegant that it genuinely stretches the imagination and is treasured by many solvers. Such clues are often discussed in the correspondence columns of daily newspapers or in the more rarefied pages of the magazine *Crossword*.

Perhaps one of the most famous is: **1** A jammed cylinder (5,4). This is a delightfully concise single-definition cryptic clue, which depends principally on a rather sticky pun on the word 'jammed'. Another, using a very similar trick is: **2** A wicked thing (6).

There are various unwritten rules about what can and can't appear in crosswords — although to some extent this is up to the discretion of the editor. By and large, anything 'distressing' or 'vulgar' (as marked in the dictionary) is usually avoided in both clues and solutions. Two of the more risqué clues to have appeared in daily newspaper puzzles were **3** What you might find at gay weddings in the isles (8) and **4** Like occupants getting down to business (9). Brand names and many of the more transient phenomena of the popular media are also deliberately avoided in most mainstream puzzles.

Of course, certain indications and devices crop up very commonly. Often seen is a variation on **5** Back door (4) — probably originally published in the *Daily Telegraph* and featured *idem in alio* in one of our own puzzles. Sometimes, compilers get very upset to see their clues reused in other puzzles, although given the ultimate limitations on how certain solutions can be constructed and the way that things tend to stick in the subconscious only to reappear as apparently original ideas, it's scarcely surprising that this should happen occasionally. One clue that caused the sparks to fly was the excellent **6** Judge taking tea-break after *Times* puzzle (8), which appeared in both *The Times* and the *FT* from different compilers.

The clues most favoured by regular solvers, however, are those which require a real leap of the imagination on either very flimsy or very misleading evidence. Try these on for size:

> **7** HIJKLMNO (5) **8** O (8,6) **9** I say nothing (3)
> **10** A stiff examination (4,6)

Answers to all these below!

1 SWISS ROLL **2** CANDLE **3** HEBRIDES [HE BRIDES] **4** SQUATTING **5** ROOD **6** ESTIMATE **7** WATER [H to O] **8** CIRCULAR LETTER **9** EGO [say] [O = EG + nothing = O] **10** POST MORTEM

Crosswords 21 – 30

Now you are on your own. Crosswords 21 – 30 contain no on-grid assistance or indications of clue devices. (Of course, all the clues are explained in detail, as usual, in the **Help for Graded Puzzles** section.)

These puzzles go from average difficulty to a standard that is probably equivalent to a prize puzzle in a weekend edition of one of the 'big' dailies. A few of the clues are quite difficult and one or two of the solutions may require the help of a dictionary to check — unless you want to look them up at the back of this book, of course!

Remember that even in a difficult crossword not *all* the clues are difficult. Look through every clue before you start, as advised in **Some Practical Advice on Solving**: you will certainly be able to get quite a few of them — which will help you tackle the tough ones.

Once you have come to terms with these crosswords, you will have encountered nearly all of the common devices used by setters in standard cryptic crosswords. You will be in a position to have a go at any of the daily paper puzzles with a fair degree of confidence. From now on, it's mainly a question of building up speed and really starting to enjoy the dazzling array of verbal deception that is displayed every day of the week on the inside or back page of your favourite newspaper.

Having conquered these crosswords you should feel confident enough to move on to the themed crosswords we include later in the book.

CROSSWORD NO. 21

ACROSS

1 Mr Fox's invitation to return to reality? (4,4,2,5)
9 Might oral constitution result in this kind of power? (9)
10 No taxi back for painter (5)
11 The last word in formal correspondence (6)
12 Help to measure extremes of company trend (8)
14 Describing parts of the body of a cat I found in derelict canal (10)
16 Forbid animal doctor to have duck (4)
18 Gloomy dean partly endorsing evangelism (4)
19 Garibaldi might be found in here! (7,3)
21 King of Sweden after August 5 revolution (8)
22 Argentine champion of a gin cocktail (6)
25 Working: not out with us, note! (2,3)
26 Source of illumination on board? (5,4)
27 Dispose of lions quickly? (2,1,7,5)

DOWN

1 Working out purpose of Will's devious brain (11,4)
2 Small contribution sounds theoretically possible (5)
3 Flash pad over prison (8)
4 Keep them about you for amusement? (4)
5 Moderate a northern church society, perhaps (10)
6 Plants firmly into foundations after measurement (6)
7 Put back in touch with Italian in revolutionary centre (9)
8 Holiday pair just hitched (9,6)
13 Fires built to create an obstruction in legislative assembly (10)
15 Bitter bark sometimes prescribed in small measure (9)
17 Light hair? (8)
20 Manage to perform twice (4,2)
23 Country store by the sound of it (5)
24 No 16 for Scottish port (4)

CROSSWORD NO. 21

CROSSWORD NO. 22

ACROSS

1 Dismiss priests for wearing this? (9)
6 Beats out old beat (5)
9 Some latent heat retained in the crucible, for example (7)
10 Anchorage found by Othello, possibly getting home at midnight (7)
11 Inert refined chemical (5)
12 Countermeasure contains nothing which responds to pressure (9)
14 Hill fort losing leader in revolt (3)
15 Bolstering up invalid as cure's near (11)
17 Eye queue reported to be greater than usual (11)
19 Drain around step (3)
20 Could be a help when changing in the gloom out East (9)
22 One kind of wood is perfect (5)
24 Clearly making a profit (7)
26 Troops not intent on evening stopover (7)
27 Of course losing equanimity initially could make one this (5)
28 Top of weapon used for frontal attack? (9)

DOWN

1 Fabric, for example, removed from seating (5)
2 He adjusted reactor (7)
3 Aspire to this in the City (9)
4 Big-headed about position (11)
5 Bad actor allowed to leave *Hamlet* (3)
6 Sweeper found in the garden (5)
7 Hit with small glove (7)
8 Enthusiasm displayed by keen Head (9)
13 Stalwart upset creeps on board (11)
14 Parts clipped off decorations (9)
16 Dog, terrier, vet almost upset (9)
18 Perhaps Del Boy runs into one of the Steptoes (7)
19 Take for granted power to start again (7)
21 Congregation gathered from Italy (5)
23 Euclid doesn't begin to be deciphered with clarity (5)
25 Gains lost in empty talk (3)

CROSSWORD NO. 22

CROSSWORD NO. 23

ACROSS

1 Meet a payment, so to speak (6)
4 Soldier following intermittent raid project makes staff officer (8)
10 French poet of the pastoral tradition? (9)
11 Failure of recess at end of trial (5)
12 Artist to draw explorer (7)
13 Sells on stories we're told (7)
14 Head's new look is a washout (5)
15 Fundamentals worried steelmen (8)
18 Casual garment suitable for those starting to drive? (3,5)
20 Philosopher introduces each of plebeian leaders as top orator (5)
23 Subject in UK National Curriculum, no doubt (7)
25 Proposition made by me to her (7)
26 Colourful addition to foundation (5)
27 Pointed proposal gets gangster overwrought (9)
28 Objectively I guard friend and fellow boarder (8)
29 Engineers defy extremes to put things right (6)

DOWN

1 Do they listen to your accounts? (8)
2 CIA leaves strict order for tank (7)
3 These may be raised by sailors celebrating on board such vessels (9)
5 Direction taken by Orpheus – and the reason he got lost! (14)
6 In the dark until decoded (5)
7 Employ a soft tip (7)
8 The first believer (6)
9 Irishmen vote Prime Minister out in state of poverty (14)
16 Dam said, for example, to be a stopgap measure (9)
17 Officially inform all youngsters (8)
19 Where you might find soldiers at breakfast time (7)
21 Called in time, upset, to settle (7)
22 Make a killing backing a famous horse (3,3)
24 Muesli nearly all regurgitated by this part of the intestine (5)

CROSSWORD NO. 23

CROSSWORD NO. 24

ACROSS

1 Bully's order to slackers in the cotton field, perhaps! (4,2)
4 Lover of 13 finds plant on mountain (8)
10 Chairs get upset in German house (9)
11 Movements D G Rossetti described as essential ingredients (5)
12 To which Browning's rider sprang (7)
13 Unruly lout is ready initially to be lover of 4 (7)
14 Naive treatment for birthmarks (5)
15 Newly named tea rose (8)
18 Returning sweets created tension (8)
20 Noticed Hancock at first in highly polished appearance (5)
23 Create order (7)
25 To sell old Spanish coin looks sound conclusion (7)
26 Empty tunnel repaired after removing last bit of obstruction (5)
27 Where a writer might settle in Barnstaple, perhaps (9)
28 Foster new line in woodland management (8)
29 Encourage doctor who's first struck off (4,2)

DOWN

1 Articulation in G Sharp composition (8)
2 French kitchen dishes (7)
3 You do things differently – like this or else! (9)
5 Sinister urge? Just the opposite! (5,4,5)
6 Begin a fight (3,2)
7 Humour could make Guildenstern back away (7)
8 Help donkey first (6)
9 Early English king and profligate poet (7,7)
16 Sober citizen briefly glimpsed in attendance (9)
17 Best bun cut up and consumed (8)
19 One taking a turn to get the drinks in? (7)
21 Summary of unfinished epic novel, for example (7)
22 Scratch around right at the back of the neck (6)
24 Has part of the bible to be translated for these (5)

CROSSWORD NO. 24

CROSSWORD NO. 25

ACROSS

1 Routine operation in the field ignoring the informer? (7,3,5)
9 Lovers abandonded all over USSR jumping into range (5)
10 River rose out of this? (9)
11 Places where parts are taken or removed? (8)
12 Base evil a Klansman covers over (6)
14 Government left in regret (4)
15 Changed direction aggrieves militant (10)
18 To get international body's support the German intervenes (10)
19 Itemize record catalogue (4)
21 Offending motorists may be subject to these vices (6)
23 One who's usually blue if you're in the red (8)
25 Girl in back seat a Roman idealizes (9)
26 Comic feast? (5)
27 Eating rot, sister suffered a nasty complaint (15)

DOWN

1 23, maybe, having a bash at self-defence (15)
2 If well-connected cosmopolitan may be so described (9)
3 On the spot, as Caesar might have been (2,4)
4 Get into the plot through this? (6,4)
5 Henry replaces top of perforated nozzle to water first part of above solution (4)
6 Lacking sense I abandoned some girls in distress (8)
7 Fragrant smell from a European capital (5)
8 Military bases where the motorist can refuel (7,8)
13 Operation which may take place in first part of 4 or 11 (10)
16 Travelling Italian tanner I upset (9)
17 Rotten part with exit on stage (4-4)
20 Doctor in South African Lancaster, for example (6)
22 Accumulate a quantity (5)
24 Produced high cheese (4)

CROSSWORD NO. 25

CROSSWORD NO. 26

ACROSS

1 Clothing acceptable in custody (6)
4 Four lines as a series (8)
10 Archangel abandoning decadent ills in claim hell is hot (7)
11 Drink disturbed editor's family (7)
12 Preparing climber, perhaps, for different position (10)
13 Cross set back in entrance (4)
15 Spectator's father finds supplement is included (7)
17 Authorize directions to count, for example (7)
19 Grey said to be one (7)
21 Scores against depleted team somewhere in Italy (7)
23 Partly send up eternal fall guy (4)
24 Copier production lacking lines on diagram (10)
27 Boy takes in stray crane (7)
28 Deprecate mean measure (7)
29 Adventurous nightlife, we're told (8)
30 French artist's entry finally discarded (6)

DOWN

1 Possibly create dam to separate areas (9)
2 Told to refer to embarrassed embraces (7)
3 Mariner is knowledgeable about craft (10)
5 Caesar felt Brutus' cut the most – this according to Antony (9)
6 Fish out relative (4)
7 Broadcast left-wing views here? (7)
8 French sculptor raised an unpleasant smell (5)
9 Scottish 11:150 to one (4)
14 Brings neat recipe for food (6-4)
16 One who splits hairs to get rid of unwelcome visitors? (9)
18 Brazilian star player rising above County in big game (9)
20 Rome, pre-Revolution, ruled by him (7)
22 Hustle using knave and king after ... (7)
23 ... a trick shuffle ... (5)
25 ... originally exposes all cards held individually (4)
26 11 briefly left in oven (4)

CROSSWORD NO. 26

CROSSWORD NO. 27

ACROSS
1 Speed party (10)
6 Accountant and politician joined clique (4)
10 Few passes for girls in these, observed Parker (7)
11 Function appropriate to hairdo clasps (7)
12 Get rid of bird nesting in flower (9)
13 Heavy poles pushed into river (5)
14 Peer obtains part-time qualification (5)
15 Hastens in order to get directions in suburb (4,5)
17 Large island's fertile region (9)
20 One the French Prime Minister backed to get things moving (5)
21 Small girl raced round outside the pits (5)
23 A fight after prison porridge (9)
25 Appear to run away from wild man-eater (7)
26 Make clergy idle round here in France (7)
27 First of all sickly and now extremely healthy (4)
28 Repent in reformed church signifying suitability (10)

DOWN
1 Keen to hear this coming up the Severn? (5)
2 President has carte blanche for drugstore philosophy (9)
3 Peter, for example, lacking final direction gets in with heretical teacher (14)
4 Will made to try tea blend (7)
5 He pours out music from his lyre (7)
7 A seed which may be found beneath an oak tree (5)
8 Does Scarlett lose her head with this swashbuckling figure? On the contrary! (9)
9 Belief in knowing where you're going before you get there (14)
14 Those who construct trains to carry royal passenger (9)
16 Former terrorists' son trapping one in blast (9)
18 Severe east wind prevailing (7)
19 High flyer allowed small morsel (7)
22 Sewer unpicked 21 (5)
24 The writer objectively supporting article's subject (5)

CROSSWORD NO. 27

CROSSWORD NO. 28

ACROSS

1 Fugitive lacking direction for hiding place ... (6)
4 ... ran away and sank without trace (8)
10 Original painter who may have been self-taught (9)
11 No way royal stutterer can be made to broadcast (5)
12 One who would love to have lied about age, no doubt! (5)
13 End bit at the foot of a page (9)
14 They cared about altered television part (7-3,4)
18 Sweet language from French blonde (7,7)
20 Clipper freeing animals from box, perhaps (9)
22 Calm down after a fit of bad temper (5)
24 Record what might be said to a knocker (5)
25 Sends one invention born before of necessity (9)
26 Class reported too soon for once (8)
27 Hit and ran (6)

DOWN

1 Reprimand professional found in range (8)
2 Overheated mate loses partner (5)
3 Good Scottish publication has English introduction for tourists (5,4)
5 Vicar might call on book-keeper to perform these (8,6)
6 Ace of hearts could be first from the bottom (5)
7 Issue concealed microphone for someone dishing the dirt! (6,3)
8 Obscure old vessel taken into study (6)
9 Very light, perhaps, a sign of trouble (8,6)
15 One instrumental in signalling four out of 6 safe (9)
16 Rambling lecture sent up musical (9)
17 Emphasized importance over senior journalist (8)
19 By this means alone (6)
21 Thrashed out eager compromise (5)
23 Alarm gets you wide-awake (5)

CROSSWORD NO. 28

CROSSWORD NO. 29

ACROSS
1 Pain from squeezing right inside tent (5)
4 Result of pile-up, in the main (9)
9 State a possible cause of 4 *Ac* (9)
10 Somewhere to drink in the vicinity (5)
11 Recognize South African instrument (6)
12 Singers rehearsing initially with no score for new arrangement (8)
14 Trying to keep fit can be worrying (10)
16 Large fish in position to dive (4)
19 Reward returning judge (4)
20 Reported naval movement keenly observed in the Middle East (5,5)
22 Carves out openings for skiing enthusiasts to fall into? (8)
23 Distressed marten flees from a trombone played by a top musician (6)
26 Painter Edward valued highly (5)
27 Cutter once pulled from rock (9)
28 Old boy fibbed about pistol, getting committed (9)
29 Dandy with inflated opinion of himself? (5)

DOWN
1 Theatre company deficit over Emu farce (9)
2 Devonian village blacksmith uses this (5)
3 Evaluate including some scenes in rehearsal (8)
4 Such laughter in part of the West End (4)
5 Grant only one involved unwittingly (10)
6 Bats may emerge from this wood (6)
7 Misplaced effort surrounding key evacuation (9)
8 'Yet each man — the thing he loves' (*Wilde*) (5)
13 Tax fools men in the street (10)
15 Three consecutive letters, say, totally at the heart of the matter (9)
17 Choose examination candidates for this process (9)
18 Are such characters encountered in strange spheres? (8)
21 Pet drink to follow (6)
22 Transport to depart with this on board? (5)
24 Sad confession before novice is sent out to indoctrinate (5)
25 Drug addiction initially supported by detectives (4)

CROSSWORD NO. 29

CROSSWORD NO. 30

ACROSS

1 Describing transport of City at a standstill (8)
6 Moody page dismissed from domestic duty (6)
9 Return a chart with an inset showing a major canal (6)
10 The queen's gunners, taking safety catch from grenade, shelled amphibian (8)
11 Poor accommodation makes young ox grow old (8)
12 Walker initially lost another (6)
13 Text detailed bonus offer (5)
14 Characteristic of mental disorder around in East (9)
17 If he's around near ark I'm tempest-tossed (9)
19 Carried away, perhaps, after a remarkable performance (8)
22 Singular French article that one is absorbed in (6)
23 One of four named in revelations (8)
24 Lead Greek character into great confusion (8)
25 Brilliant article I malign (6)
26 Regretting having broken firm's first universal rule (6)
27 Old records American decisively beats (8)

DOWN

2 Boisterous tea circle briefly upset citizen (7)
3 Great Dani may be misprint for this dramatic figure! (9)
4 Sparkling headgear often worn by rulers ... (6)
5 ... one of whom once mobilized support for fiery revolutionaries (9,6)
6 Peg's proper name (8)
7 Urge disobedient child over fashionable university (7)
8 Founder of classes over the hill (9)
13 Operating surgeon takes councillor a sponge (9)
15 Bossy maiden created a fluster (9)
16 Serge may be third character promoted in 15 according to Shakespeare (8)
18 Take off limit at Entebbe is more than adequate (7)
20 Count this before drinking, perhaps – his victims afterwards? (7)
21 Old trains not working produce anger (6)

CROSSWORD NO. 30

Beyond the Black-and-White Grid

At various points in the text, we have mentioned the fact that more complex crosswords exist — such as those that appear in various sections of *The Observer* and the *Sunday Times*. These puzzles, particularly the one by Jonathan Crowther ('AZED') in the *Observer*, develop traditions started by three famous crossword-setters, Torquemada, Afrit and Ximenes. (Ximenes — Derrick Macnutt — was responsible for laying down much of the 'ethical' basis of clue-writing and diagram construction in his book *Ximenes on the Art of the Crossword*.)

The most obvious difference between the so-called 'advanced' cryptic and the ordinary daily crossword is that the advanced variety uses a completely different style of diagram: the barred grid. Instead of black squares, the divisions between solutions are marked on the grid with bars. The barred grid usually contains fewer squares (12 x 12 as opposed to 15 x 15) but all of the squares are filled when the puzzle is completed. This gives the crossword a rather daunting appearance, although it should be pointed out that there are fewer 'unches' (unchecked squares) than in most conventional diagrams, thus giving the solver a greater chance of working out answers to some of the more diabolical clues — provided, of course, that the 'straightforward' ones have already been solved!

The level of vocabulary required to solve an advanced cryptic is such that a dictionary (*Chambers* is almost invariably recommended) is essential. Both solutions and clues can contain highly obscure words or archaic usages, although setters usually try to obey one of the golden Ximenean rules, whereby a difficult solution should have a (relatively) easy clue.

Advanced cryptics still contain most, if not all, of the devices that we have described in this book. However, many of the indications (of anagrams, for instance) are much more sophisticated, and the range of abbreviations and 'crossword speak' is also considerably more varied.

As with any art form, practitioners, setters and solvers alike, are constantly striving to extend the possibilities of the crossword. One method is the themed puzzle.

Themed puzzles are usually titled and are provided with a preamble explaining what is required of the solver. The title should confirm that the solver has got the right idea. The 'Enigmatic Variations' series in the *Sunday Telegraph* has the tradition of repeating the title in the preamble, as demonstrated in QUADRANTS, one of the puzzles mentioned below.

Following this chapter we have provided four examples of the more straightforward types of themed puzzle. Do not be daunted from reading on. Now that you have mastered the basic rules and frameworks detailed in this book you are capable of going further. In the words of the late Michael Rich, former editor of the 'Listener' puzzle, advanced cryptics 'are not elitist, they are just harder'.

The following paragraphs are by no means a complete description of these crossword developments. They are designed as an introduction to whet your appetite.

Most grids in themed puzzles are barred and in the format described above. The exception is the 'Listener' puzzle, now appearing in the *Saturday Times*. There the shape of the grid may vary, as appropriate to the theme. Some are circular and at least one has represented a map of the UK mainland. In this book we will not develop this, but it is an indication of how setters' imaginations are constantly being extended.

Whilst clueing still obeys the basic rules, there are some different elements introduced. These may be, for example, the inclusion of superfluous words or misprints. In our examples we have kept the clueing straightforward. The one exception to this is the clue without definition which appears in SOMETHING TO WORRY OVER. In this type of clue the subsidiary indications follow the normal rules, but there is no definition included. There is usually a batch of these clues producing answers which are all of a kind, and which, if defined, would give the game away.

The method of entry into the grid may be varied. Sometimes, as in three of the following puzzles, answers must be amended before entry. Some answers may be required to be jumbled or reversed. Another variant is the letters latent device, where one letter is removed from the answer before entry, the subsidiary indications also leaving out this letter. We have not used these methods. Amendments to grid entries may involve the resolution of clashes between checked letters. Where such letters are not the same solvers must decide on the correct entry, in line with the deduced theme of the crossword. This device has been used in two of the following puzzles. In SOMETHING TO WORRY OVER solvers are required to deduce where and how eight answers are to be entered.

Many puzzles, eg those in *The Spectator,* use unclued lights.

These are generally a group of words linked to the theme suggested by the title. Just one example is included in SOMETHING TO WORRY OVER and in CHANGING SIDES; and there are two in JAYWALKING. Perimeters (the squares around the edge of the grid) are sometimes unclued and contain quotations or relevant phrases.

Messages may be hidden or otherwise given in the completed grid, as in CHANGING SIDES. These are usually hidden in a straight line, either diagonally, vertically or horizontally, and will often make use of the centre of the grid. It is not considered fair to hide short words, although this was done in JAYWALKING, in which there is a group of hidden words, one of which occupies most of a complete column. It is possible to solve this puzzle correctly without finding them all. The different elements introduced into the clueing mentioned above are usually used to spell out a relevant message which may be an instruction. The initial letters of superfluous words are an example of this. Single unclued lights, as in SOMETHING TO WORRY OVER, may also be used as such. This is also the purpose of the letters latent device previously described.

Setters often give themselves additional challenges not always obvious to the solver, but invariably helpful when spotted. One of these is the pangram, where each letter of the alphabet has been used at least once. Spotting which of the following four puzzles is one should help with solving some of the more obscure words. Discerning another variant is essential to providing the correct lights in one of the other puzzles.

In advanced cryptics there is often something else to be done after the grid has been completed. The most common of these is highlighting, as in CHANGING SIDES. Sometimes, however, something has to be altered. This is not the only reason it is advisable to use a pencil! Indeed, one puzzle, entitled 'Use A Pencil' in the 'Listener' series, bore the coded message 'Erase everything and send in blank'.

Anyone wishing to explore these areas further can do no better than consult Don Manley's *Chambers Crossword Manual*, which contains a detailed description of the features of advanced cryptics, together with a large number of sample puzzles.

Themed puzzles of the nature we have described currently appear in the *Independent on Saturday*, *Sunday Telegraph* and the 'Listener' puzzle in the *Saturday Times*. This latter was described by Leonard Bernstein as 'the best crossword in the world. I never miss it'. The weekly *Spectator* features the specific variety mentioned earlier. Specialist monthly magazines include *Crossword*, the magazine of the Crossword Club. Details are given in **Further Reading and Contacts**. We recommend you begin with the *Independent on Saturday*.

Finally, a word about setters. Pseudonyms are always used, eg MORDRED (Derrick), EMKAY (Michael Kindred), and GANDER (Georgie and Derrick). As mentioned elsewhere, we get to know the work of some of the best and look forward to their puzzles with a mixture of eager anticipation and trepidation.

In order to provide the maximum variety the publications mentioned above have limits on the time span between each setter's submissions, usually about six months.

Do pursue themed crosswords. They are fun.

Themed Puzzles

Now we come to the final set of puzzles. These are typical of those one might find in the weekend section of the broadsheet newspapers. They are harder than normal cryptics but certainly within your powers if you've got this far. We hope you will experience the penny-dropping moments which will reveal the themes. The help section for these puzzles provides assistance with the answers, but you are still required to deduce methods of entry — these are given with the solutions.

CHANGING SIDES by Gander

ACROSS
1 Cure some pig's trotter, reportedly (4)
5 Intense, determined description of eyes (7)
10 King Erik booed lax playing (8)
12 Poke around Dutch village (4)
13 Thrash retreating general, a worm (8)
16 Plant variety of Arabian seed (6)
17 Fools eating 50 crows (6)
19 Girl has to search around for sponge (9)
21 Where one might be served French coffee with meal in American state (9)
24 Fish service pinched by sailors (6)
25 Bright copper turned in fast (6)
26 I'll say you are hard (4)
29 Main weedkiller bringing cold comfort initially for 500 fish (8)
30 Arab by a long sea (4)
31 Disagreed and extravagantly defied father (8)
32 Initially relish, say, Miss Hari's fruits (7)
33 Like a fish eye lens, originally the ultimate in photography (4)

DOWN
1 Spanish gentleman made Hilda be pregnant (7)
2 Everybody loves a primitive lizard (8)
3 Gazelle, possibly, taking off before long striding run (4)
4 60s teenagers taking exercise with scooters (6)
6 Placid people see orgy as dissolute (9)
7 Spenser's to destroy last of malodour in former dump (6)
8 Leaders of Shetland kinsmen encircle Orcadian outbuilding (4)
9 Reported time for dead writ (4)
11 Under fire in France, the band's putting spears away (8)
14 Eastern disease starts to ravage Indonesians after insect bites wife (8)
15 Where violinist may have his hands with drink to swallow (9)
18 Support for one in the cart? (8)
20 Note score having decisive effect (7)
22 Sterility appals at first before first-rate bed turns up (6)
23 Wooden artefacts including acceptable dish (6)
26 Betrayal literally is too much for second person in S Carolina (4)
27 Eagerly beheaded giant (4)
28 Staminate tree towering around Australia (4)

CHANGING SIDES by Gander

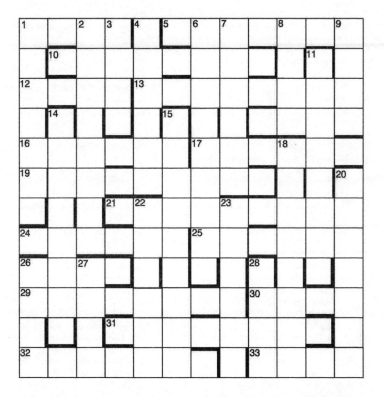

A number of answers require treatment before entry into the grid. Clarification of this is to be found hidden in the completed grid. The message so given provides an alternative title and should be highlighted. Although there are various possibilities for completion of the unclued light, consideration of the theme should enable solvers to deduce the correct letter.

Gander is a collaboration between Derrick Knight and Georgie Johnson, MORGAN of the *Independent on Saturday.* Georgie also works jointly with other setters, notably Jim Snell, otherwise known as Ix, who contributes to all the advanced cryptic publications mentioned. Their pseudonym is MORIX.

QUADRANTS by Mordred

ACROSS
1 Spike hair curl (7)
2 Old tapestry conservationists have left so much the worse (5)
9 The railway post circuit en route to Edinburgh from King's Cross? (9)
11 Ae leaving to arrange transfer – old property? (6)
13 Pole smashed Greek jug (4)
14 Somewhat slipshod Japanese religious leader (5)
16 Bear hard time (4)
17 Indian's respectful term for first one in tent (4)
19 Former sex symbol has no time for Buddhist stage (5)
22 Rose, exploiting members, thrown out of pub (8)
24 I throw out a hollow case for how prism is formed (8)
25 Strangely, perhaps, evens bet has no appeal (5)
28 Wet Westminster politician (4)
30 Here raw recruit bowled out American fool (4)
32 I probe avidly into social workers' residential provision (5)
34 Worthless Australian fiat possibly revoked (4)
35 Brass-founder worked intricate frond cast in a series of mouldings (7)
36 State international baccalaureate held by one leading emeritus initially may be disregarded (9)
37 Faustus, ultimately, is not a soul in heaven (5)
38 Exercise routine leaving soldiers short of time (7)

DOWN
1 Edmund's caught jack finally leaving crew (5)
2 Pike, maybe one caught by angler (4)
3 Row about dry oil (5)
4 Dog food (8)
5 Transactions with extremely exorbitant allowance for waste (4)
6 Kanaka's farewell call you hear intermittently (5)
7 Take in policy revision concerning an internal opening (7)
8 Scoot up north elevating unknown party head (7)
10 Covering letter about the German military intelligence (9)
12 Sketch in crude crayon perhaps (9)
15 Elegant Scots journal replaces 28's leader (4)
18 Look hard on river for inflatable structure (8)
20 'Tis sour coming to grief (7)
21 Prig served in charge of independence (7)
23 UN chief sent up Australian fool (4)
26 Hounds of Hell finally yowl after Mephistopheles, straining leads (5)
27 Stalk numberless horses (5)
29 Try kissing new groom (5)
31 Miss in love with German (5)
33 Lamp lit tree (5)

QUADRANTS by Mordred

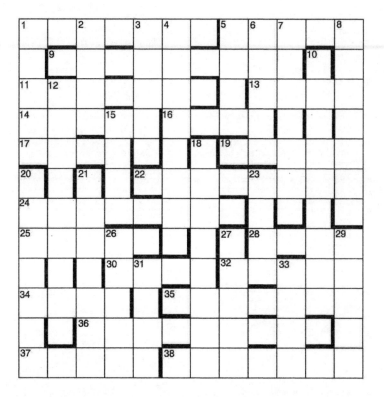

Ten answers are to be modified before entry into the grid. The lights thus formed are all real words, except for one abbreviation, known worldwide. In three cases this resolves clashes; in two there is a clash where neither clashing letter is entered; in four there is no clash; and in one the modification occurs in an unchecked square. Close examination of the placement of entries in QUADRANTS is recommended, as is *The Chambers Dictionary.*

SOMETHING TO WORRY OVER by Mordred

Clues without Definition

Leading player, Terry, forgetting lines (7)

Run in fratricide (5)

Backward looking mug takes back former spouse (5)

Easy Street (5)

Russia welcoming foreign aid (6)

Sailor's suspicious behaviour (5)

Part of Hebridean village (5)

Appearing in court after first of remands in prison (7)

ACROSS

10 Maria cut short playing this role? (4)
11 Chief priest, heretic originally, in time runs church (8)
12 I use an improvised cosh and initially break into potter's box (10)
14 Tonite, oddly, explosive (3)
16 Rarely decent reactionary name overwhelms Henry (5)
19 Reported fall costly for Rudolph, perhaps (8)
22 Railway; a line which may take you to Tel Aviv (4)
26 Plant mother leaves 19 possibly (4)
27 Inflammation explosions requiring two separate iodine injections (8)
30 Seduction as contrived arrangement involving an X (11)
34 Hill-dweller's incomplete earthwork (5)
35 Remnant of burning tree (3)
38 One enjoying the high life filling old city with triumphant cries (8)
39 Artist's retrospective to be in Paris (4)

DOWN

1 One in order, first in series (6)
2 Block hospital's abandoned through passage (6)
3 More than one spoke of Princess briefly captivated by pop music (5)
4 Oxford scholar barred at broadcast (8)
5 Objectively, we head support for fair game's excellent quality (13)
6 A germ could develop into a fruit (5)
7 Violin soaring in swift movements (5)
8 Upset blackcurrant drink king's dropped (3)
9 Unfortunately he lacks restraint (7)
13 Indian peasant, somewhere in Bombay, rising (5)
15 Cut scythe handle (4)
17 First of all houses usually laugh over this eponymous French holidaymaker (5)
20 I struggled, entwined by a creeper (5)
21 Seasoned beef in batter with mostly crusty savoury coating (7)
24 Put finger on this up to a point? (5)
25 Greece accepted British vessel (4)
28 Popular pose acceptable in first place (6, two words)
29 Hard slog for school pupil overcoming old record (6)
31 He investigated New World claret, firstly one bottle (5)
32 King is exalted pack leader (5)
33 Private meal with no starter (5)
36 What's left of right? (3)

SOMETHING TO WORRY OVER by Mordred

Eight answers are clued without definition. Solvers are required to deduce the links between them and where and how they should be entered. The unclued light at 23 Across (a four word phrase) should help with this. [The puzzle has been created with only two unchecked letters in 23 Across in order to provide some assistance to new solvers, who will also notice that there are twice as many unclued lights as there are spaces for them.]

JAYWALKING by Mordred

(Originally published in *Tough Crosswords*, March, 2001)

ACROSS
1 Pushes prams to give an example
5 Magistrates extremely exasperated by convoluted lies
10 Soldiers tense following defensive measures after escape from fortification
11 Dido forsaking divinity for dabble in Tyre
12 Donation of land with a fixity of tenure perhaps? Without question
13 Women's guardian arresting the plotters
14 Roman reciter not to be taken seriously
16 These marchers were in conflict with employment endlessly receding
18 Hesistate to bid, therefore...
19 ... deliberately lose the lead to former player
20 Scotsman, unsurprisingly, finds penny scant in Aberdeen
22 Beam is dropping, needing new weld maybe
23 Regulate to make advantage fair
25 Clothing giving Australian cricketers the fidgets?
30 No end to lost baggage on Queen Elizabeth possibly making you stomp
31 Radical liberal follower of Johnson perhaps
32 Corneal deposit's unacceptable discharges
33 Lover putting on weight with bump
34 Uncertainty about retreating army's order
36 Nazarene's reverberating call to prayer
37 Soldier abandoning uniform for unarmed combat
38 Wad put on treble about to be returned to heavy gamber
39 Steep run once taking time
40 Telegraph leader's sequel to animated press broadcast of yesterday

DOWN
1 Tired old hack is retired
2 Quartz-like mineral reportedly turning up in cotton states
3 Some shilly-shallying as to naming a Frenchman
4 Fasten crystal box
6 It's handy taking one to remove oil
7 Wrongs by law settled in bars formerly
8 No more black coal
9 Bodyguard eating Desperate Dan's dinner that is missing capers
12 Know Shakespeare's shrew Kate? Tameable termagant fundamentally
15 They're meant to be helpful but said to be awkward
17 Score run overcoming appeal
21 Rose screamed out wanting Italian girl to be a Spanish one
23 Egyptian god with ram's head, no tail, and arms
24 Language of France adopted by Afghan
25 Action replay facility shows number ten is in
26 Flier dropping in for a drink? Quite the reverse
27 Armstrong maybe making a walk up in the moon
28 *The Scotsman*'s short clever supporting piece from hack
29 Accompany an explorer picking up points
31 With a mild oath he raised a saw
33 Sounder males: no bachelor blades
35 First person in Versailles transporting girl up to dance

JAYWALKING by Mordred

(Originally published in *Tough Crosswords*, March, 2001)

The two unclued lights represent (a) a slang generic term, thematically treated, and (b) a specific example in which the offender meets his inevitable fate. Another generic term of which seven specific examples appear in the grid, should be highlighted by the solver. [The preceding sentences reproduce the original preamble. Our solvers may ignore the last sentence, unless they wish to have a go — it is a three-letter word and therefore would not be deemed fair in most circles. Here the solver is required to deduce what has happened to the entries where the answers won't fit and to demonstrate a full understanding of the theme by completing the unclued lights. One light may be found in *The Times Atlas*. Other words are in *The Chambers Dictionary*.]

Two-way Crossword Glossary

Where does 'flower' become 'river', 'spanner' become 'bridge', and 'lower' become 'cow'? In the devious minds of cryptic crossword setters! In setting puzzles, they aim to please, entertain and perplex, all in a legitimate way, of course. They do this, in part, by including in some of their clues words and phrases which translate into meanings and abbreviations which are not necessarily defined as such in an everyday dictionary. So, 'flower' is thought of as something which flows, 'spanner' as something which spans, and 'lower' as something which lows. The main purpose of this glossary (which is not meant to be exhaustive) is to help solvers become more familiar with this cryptic 'crossword speak'.

An example of this is the word 'sailor', which in a clue could mean 'MARINER', 'YACHTSMAN', 'AB' (Able Seaman), 'OS' (Ordinary Seaman), 'JACK' or 'TAR'. It might also be alluding to a famous sailor in real life such as 'DRAKE' or 'NELSON', or in fiction to 'LONG JOHN SILVER' or 'HORNBLOWER'.

We have described the glossary as 'two-way', because you can look up, for instance, DOCTOR, and one of the alternatives is 'GP'. If you look up GP, one of the meanings listed is 'doctor'. We have not carried this facility to the nth degree as it could swell the glossary to become a small dictionary in its own right — which is outside the scope of our book.

Some of the entries include indications of how words may be used to show the kinds of devices employed by the setter, and also instructions as to what to do with certain parts of a clue. For example, under 'IN' is found 'indicates letters within a word'. So, if you came across a clue which read 'Animal in classroom (3)', the word 'in' in this case would be telling you to look for the name of an animal in the word 'classroom', the answer being 'ASS'. (The number at the end of the clue indicates the number of letters in the answer.)

Under some words is 'any example'. If you look at 'ELEMENT', you will see that we have put 'any chemical element' and listed a couple of them. To list all the elements would take up too much room! We have, however, included all the International Vehicle Registrations (IVRs) — also known as International Car Index Marks — as it is harder to find a reference book in which these are given.

We have not specifically listed anagram indicators, as there are so many of them! Almost any word which indicates movement, replacement, change, or re-sorting is permissible. Some of the words in the glossary, however, may also serve as anagram indicators and these are marked with an asterisk (*). We would like to mention two of them which seem unlikely candidates: 'ON' in a theatrical sense means 'playing' which indicates movement, and 'OUT' which can mean 'away from the original or normal position'.

In common with modern practice, we have omitted full stops from abbreviations, and we have not generally shown accents and apostrophes (normally ignored in answers to clues), as all of these could distract the solver from making progress in using the glossary to help solve a clue.

We have included some meanings or equivalents which we don't think are entirely legitimate, but which, nevertheless, you will come across in some of the puzzles in the national dailies. There are no rules and regulations set in stone for use by setters; there are guidelines in various books, and these vary according to who is the author.

If you make an effort to become familiar with as much of this cryptic crossword language as possible, you will gradually avoid being misled by the setter, who would invite you to see only the conventional meanings of words in clues.

Have fun!

A

A ace, adult, alpha, amateur, an, ante, argon, article, Austria, best, first (letter), first class, high class, I (= 1), key, note, one, per

AA abstainers, ack-ack, Alcoholics Anonymous, anti-aircraft, Automobile Association, flak, non-drinkers

AB able(-bodied) seaman, backward scholar, Jack, mariner, ordinary seaman, rating, sailor

ABANDONED* left (out)

ABB abbess, abbey, abbot

ABE Lincoln (Abraham)

ABLE fit

ABLE(-BODIED) SEAMAN AB

ABOARD at sea, on board, *indicates letter(s) between* 'SS'

ABOUT* approximate, around, c, ca, on, re, *indicates reversal of letters, letters surrounding*

ABOVE over, *indicates letter(s) positioned above*

ABSTAINERS AA, non-drinkers, teetotallers, TTs

AC account, air(crafts)man, (alternating) current, bill

ACCEPTABLE OK, U

ACCOUNT ac, story, tale

ACCOUNTANT CA

ACE A, best, card, expert, first class, I (= 1), master, one, service

ACK-ACK AA (anti-aircraft)

ACTOR ham (poor actor), player, thespian *any example*: Tree, *etc*

ACTORS cast

AD advertisement, anno Domini, announcement, notice, nowadays, poster, the present

ADDER counter, viper

ADD(ITION) PPS, PS, *indicates letter(s) added*

ADM Admiral, officer

ADMIRAL Adm, *any example*: Nelson *etc*

ADN Yemen

ADO* fuss

ADULT A

ADVERTISEMENT ad

AFG Afghanistan

AFGHANISTAN AFG

AFLOAT on board, *indicates letter(s) between* 'SS'

A FRENCH un, une

AFTERNOON pm, post meridiem

AFTERTHOUGHT postscript, PPS, PS

AG silver

AGAINST anti, con, v, versus, vs, *indicates letter(s) adjoining*

AGE era, eon, epoch, period, time

AGENT G-man, rep, representative, spy

AGENTS CIA, G-men

A GERMAN ein, eine

AI (= A1) best, capital, elite, excellent, first class, high class, sloth (ai)

AIR appearance, bearing, display, element, look, mien, tune

AIRFORCE RAF, RFC

AIRMAN AC, flier/flyer, FO (Flight Officer), PO (Pilot Officer), *any example of wind player*: oboist, trumpeter, *etc*

AIRMEN RAF, Royal Air Force

AIT island (small)

AL Alabama, Albania, aluminium, boy's name, gangster (Capone)

A LA to the French

ALABAMA Al

ALBANIA AL

ALCOHOL *any example*: brandy, gin, wine, *etc*

ALCOHOLICS ANONYMOUS AA

ALDERNEY GBA

ALECTO Fury

ALGERIA DZ

ALIEN* ET

ALL RIGHT okay, U

ALLY associate, friend, mate, pal

ALPHA A, first, IST (= 1st)

(ALTERNATING) CURRENT AC

ALTERNATIVE(LY) or

ALUMINIUM Al

ALWAYS e(v)er

AM American, backward scholar, early, morning

AMATEUR A, L (learner), tyro

AMBASSADOR Excellency, HE

AMEN last word

AMERICA(N) Am, US, USA, Uncle Sam, Yank, Yankee

(AMERICAN) SOLDIER GI

AMONG inter, *indicates hidden word, letters placed within word*

AMPUTATED cut, *indicates deletion of letter(s)*

AN a, article, I (= 1), if, one

ANAESTHETIC number

ANCIENT Iago, old, *indicates obsolete spelling*

AND Andorra

AND FRENCH et

ANDORRA AND

AND OTHERS et al

ANGER* ire, rage

ANGLE fish, L

ANNO DOMINI AD

ANNOUNCEMENT ad

ANON anonymous, soon, shortly, prolific poet

ANONYMOUS anon

ANT insect, (social) worker

ANTE a, before

ANTI against, con, v, versus, vs

ANTI-AIRCRAFT AA, ack-ack, flak

APPRENTICE L

APPROX(IMATE) about

APRIL March past

AQ water

ARAMIS Musketeer

ARCH spanner

ARCHER bowman, bridge, Cupid, Dan, Eros, Hood, Tell

ARGENTINA RA

ARGON A

ARIES heavenly body, ram

ARM branch, limb, member

ARMY soldiers, SA, TA, *etc*

AROUND* about, c, *indicates letters surrounding*

ARRIVAL TIME birth, ETA

ARSENAL gunners, RA

ART article, boy's name, painting

ARTICLE a, an, art, the

ARTILLERY cannon, guns, RA, weapons

ARTIST painter, RA, *any example*: Bacon, Tiepolo, *etc*

AS qua

ASHEN pale, wan

ASS association

ASSENT ay(e)

ASSOCIATE ally, pal

ASSOCIATION ass

ASSUME don

ATE goddess

AT HOME in, not out

ATHOS Musketeer

ATROPOS Fate

AT SEA* aboard, *indicates letter(s) within* 'SS' (steamship)

ATTORNEY DA

AT UNIVERSITY up

AU gold, to the French

AUDIENCE house

AUS Australia

AUSTRALIA Aus, Oz

AUSTRIA A

AUTHOR pen, writer, *any example*: Swift, Wells, *etc*

AUTO automatic, car

AUTOMATIC auto

AUTOMOBILE ASSOCIATION AA

AV avenue, average, bible (Authorized Version), way

AVE avenue, average, hail, way, welcome

AVENUE av, ave, road, way

AVERAGE av, ave

AWAY gone off, *indicates removal of letter(s)*

AY(E) assent

B

B bachelor, baron, Belgium, beta, bishop, black, book, born, bowled, breadth, British, bye, extra, key, note

BA Bachelor of Arts, barium, degree, graduate, scholar

BACHELOR B

BACHELOR OF ARTS BA

BACHELOR OF MEDICINE MB

BACK bet, second, stern, support, *indicates reversal of letters*

BACKWARDS *indicates reversal of letters*

BACKWARD SCHOLAR AB, AM

BACON artist, author, ham

BAHAMAS BS

BAHRAIN BRN

BALL beamer, bouncer, delivery, O

BANGER car, firework, gun, sausage

BANGLADESH BD

BAR counter, obstacle, pub, save

BARBADOS BDS

BARD Shakespeare

BARIUM Ba

BARON B, joint

BARONET Bart, Bt

BART Baronet, Lionel

BASE METAL lead

BATTING in, not out

BB bed and breakfast, books, Boys' Brigade, Brigitte Bardot, very black/soft (pencil)

BC before Christ, British Columbia

BD Bangladesh

BDS Barbados

BEAK bill, judge, magistrate, master, nose, pecker, teacher

BEAMER ball, delivery

BEAR ean

BEARING air, appearance, aspect, carriage, direction (N, E, S, W, NE, *etc*), look, port, *indicates containing letter(s) or support of letter(s) above*

BEARS has

BECK brook, rill, stream

BED cot

BED AND BREAKFAST B (and) B

BEE buzzer, drone, insect, worker

BEETLE Volkswagen, VW

BEFORE ante, ere

BEFORE CHRIST BC

BEGINNER deb, L, tiro, tyro

BELARUS SU

BELGIUM B

BELIZE BH

BELOW sub, *indicates letters placed below*

BENIN DY

BENT grass

BESIEGE invest, *indicates letter(s) within a word*

BEST A, AI (= A1), ace

BET back

BETA B

BETTING SP

BETWEEN inter, *indicates hidden word*

BG Bulgaria

BH Belize

BIBLE AV, NT, OT, RV

BIH Bosnia Herzegovina

BIKE RACE TT (Tourist Trophy)

BILL ac, Will

BIRD flier, winger, *any example*: hen, rook, swift, *etc*

BIRTH arrival time

BISHOP B, Bp, (chess)man, church-man, RR, piece on (chess) board

BK book

BLACK B, sable

BLOOMER flower (*any example*: daisy, pink, *etc*)

BLOOMING out

BLOWER phone

BLUE Conservative, down, low, sad, Tory

BM (British) Museum

BO body odour, holy tree

BOARD (company) directors, em-bark, food, keep, table

BOAT E, ship, SS, U, vessel, yacht

BOB hairstyle, s (shilling), uncle

BOBBY PC

BODYGUARD SS (Hitler's)

BODY ODOUR BO

BOOK b, bk, enter, reserve, tome, vol, volume

BOOKS bb, NT, OT

BORN b, n, nat, né, née

BOSNIA HERZEGOVINA BIH

BOTSWANA RB

BOUNCER ball, delivery

BOUNDARY four (IV), six (VI)

BOW play (violin, *etc*)

BOWLED b, delivered

BOWMAN archer, fiddler, Cupid, Eros, Hood, Tell, violinist

BOXER Chinese, dog, *any example*: Clay, Dempsey, *etc*, *or* heavyweight, flyweight, *etc*

BOY lad, son, *any (usually shor-tened) example*: Al, Sam, Tom, *etc*

BOYS' BRIGADE BB

BP Bishop

BR branch, Brazil, bridge, Britain, British, British Rail, brother, brown, lines, railway, trains

BRA (female) support(er)

BRADMAN Don

BRANCH arm, Br

BRASS cash, money

BRAZIL BR

BREADTH b

BREAK* *indicates letter(s) within word*

BRIDGE archer, br, rest, spanner

BRIDGE PLAYERS N, S, E, W

BRIG brigadier, officer, prison

BRIGITTE BARDOT BB

BRITAIN Br, GB

BRITISH B, Br

BRITISH COLUMBIA BC

BRITISH MUSEUM BM
BRITISH RAIL BR
BRN Bahrain
BRO brother
BROOK beck, flower, rill, Sir Peter, stream, tolerate
BROTHER Br, Bro, Fra, monk
BROWN br
BRU Brunei
BRUNEI BRU
BS Bahamas
BT baronet
BULGARIA BG
BUR Myanmar (Burma)
BURMA (MYANMAR) BUR
BURNS Scottish flowers
BURUNDI RU
BURY entomb, inter
BUTLER RAB
BUTTER goat, ram, person who hesitates
BUZZER bee
BYE b, extra

C

C about, approximate, around, carbon, caught, celsius, cent, century, chapter, circa, cold, Conservative, Cuba, hundred, key, note, large number, many, ton, Tory
CA about, calcium, California, (Chartered) Accountant, circa
CAL California
CALCIUM Ca
CALIF California
CALIFORNIA CA, Cal, Calif
CALLIOPE Muse
CAMBODIA K
CAN is able, preserve, tin, vessel
CANADA CDN
CANNON artillery
CANVAS sail, tent

CAP hat, lid, officer, top
CAPE cloak, head(land)
CAPITAL AI (= A1), *any example*: Paris, *etc*
CAPITALS Caps
CAPS capitals, *indicates letters going above*
CAPTAIN Capt, master, skipper, *any example*: Hornblower, *etc*
CAR auto, banger
CARBON C
CARD humorous character, *any example*: Ace, Heart, *etc*
CARE OF co
CARRIAGE bearing, port, trap, *any example*: hansom, phaeton, *etc*
CARRY FORWARD cf
CARTOONIST *any example*: Gilray, Low, *etc*
CASE *any example*: acc(usative), nom(inative), *etc*
CASH brass, money, tin
CASH ON DELIVERY cod
CAST actors, company, players
CASTLE (chess)man, chess piece, R, rook
CAT *any example*: lion, ounce, *etc*
CATTLE kine, neat, oxen
CAUGHT c, ct, dismissed, snagged
CDN Canada
CE Church (of England), (Civil) Engineer
CELEBRITY VIP
CELSIUS C
CENT c, century, coin
CENTRAL key, *indicates the middle of a word*
CENTRAL AFRICAN REPUBLIC RCA
CENTRAL HEATING ch
CENTURY c, cent, hundred, ton
CF carried forward, compare
CH central heating, chapter, child, China, church, Companion (of Honour), Switzerland

CHA tea, *sounds like*: char

CHANNEL ISLANDS CI

CHAP chapter

CHAPTER c, ch, chap, section

CHAR daily, do, home help, tea

CHARGE ion

CHARTERED ACCOUNTANT CA

CHE Guevara, revolutionary

CHEAT do

CHEF cook

CHESSMAN/PIECE bishop, castle, king, knight, man, pawn, queen, rook

CHIEF OFFICER CO

CHILD ch, imp, issue, tot

CHILE RCH

CHINA Ch, *any example*: Dresden, *etc*

CHINESE oriental, *any dynasty*: Ming, Tang, *etc*

CHLORINE Cl

CHRISTMAS present time

CHROMIUM Cr

CHROMOSOME X, Y

CHURCH CE, Ch, RC

CHURCHMAN DD, father, *any office-holder*: (arch)bishop, *etc*

CHURCH OF ENGLAND CE

CI Channel Islands, Côte d'Ivoire

CIA agents, spies

CID detectives, Spanish hero, Yard

CIRCA c, ca

CIRCLE O, ring

CIRCUIT O

CIT citizen

CITIZEN cit

CITY EC, *any example*: Ely, Rome, *etc*

CIVIL ENGINEER CE

CL chlorine, Sri Lanka

CLERGY cloth, priests

CLINK gaol, jail

CLIO Muse

CLOTH clergy, priests, *any material*: drill, serge, *etc*

CLOTHO Fate

CLUB card, *any golf club*: driver, iron, *etc, any institution*: Athenaeum, MCC, RAC, Tottenham, Villa, *etc*

CO care of, Colombia, Colorado, Commanding Officer, company, county

COB swan

COCKNEY *indicates imitation of Cockney pronunciation, such as dropped aitch*

COD cash on delivery, fish

COIN *any example*: cent, nickel, penny (p, d), quarter, shilling, *etc*

COINS currency, *plurals of above*

COL Colonel, Colorado, column, officer, pass, neck

COLOMBIA CO

COLONEL Col, officer

COLORADO CO, Col

COLUMN col

COME BACK *indicates reversal of letters*

COMMANDING OFFICER CO

COMPANION CH (of Honour)

COMPANY co

COMPARE cf

COMPOSER writer, *any example*: Britten, Ireland, *etc*

CON against, anti, Conservative, party, politician, study, Tory, with Italian

CONCERNING over

CONGO RCB

CONGO, DEMOCRATIC RE-PUBLIC OF ZRE

CONSERVATIVE blue, C, Con, party, politician, Tory

CONSTANT H, K

COOK* chef, fiddle, explorer, *any method*: boil, fry, grill, stew, *etc*

COPPER bobby, Cu, PC, peeler, penny (d, p)

CORNER turn

CORPORAL Corp, NCO, non-commissioned officer, Nym

COS cosine, island, lettuce

COSINE cos

COSTA RICA CR

COT bed, cottage, house

CÔTE D'IVOIRE CI

COTTAGE cot, house

COUNT Dracula

COUNTER adder, bar

COURSE direction (N, S, E, W, NE, *etc*), *any food course*

COW lower, neat

CPL Corporal, non-commissioned officer

CR chromium, Costa Rica, credit

CRAZY* mad

CREDIT cr

CREW eight, oarsmen

CRICKET SIDE eleven, leg, off, on, XI

CRITICISM flak

CROATIA HR

CROSS* hybrid, irate, X, *any example*: zo, tau, *etc*

CRY greet

CS Civil Service, (poison) gas

CT caught

CU copper

CUBA C

CUPID archer, bowman, Eros, love

CURRENCY coins, notes, *any example*: dollars, lira, yen, *etc*

CURRENT AC, DC

CUT amputated, *indicates letter(s) removed*

CY Cyprus

CYPRUS CY

CZ Czech Republic

CZECH REPUBLIC CZ

D

D copper, daughter, day, dead, delta, died, duke, Germany, key, late, many, note, (old) penny

DA District Attorney

DAB expert, fish, master

DAD Fr, generator, pa, pop

DAILY char, home help, *any newspaper*: *Times*, *etc*

DAM mother

DAN Archer

DANCE* ball, measure, *any example*: hop, twist, *etc*

DAS, DER, DIE the German

DAUGHTER d

DAY d, *any day or abbreviation*: Mon, Wed, Sun, *etc*

DC current

DD churchman, Doctor of Divinity

DE (DE LA, DES, DU) of the French

DEAD d, ex, late, over

DEAN Inge

DEB beginner, debutante, girl, L, one coming out

DEBT(S) IOU(S)

DEBTOR dr

DEBUTANTE deb, one coming out

DEC deceased, December, declared, last month, ult

DECEMBER Dec, last month

DECLARED dec

DECORATION *any example*: MC, MBE, OBE, *etc*

DEEP sea

DEGREE BA, *etc*

DELIVERED bowled

DELIVERY ball, beamer, bouncer

DELTA D

DEN lair, retreat, study

DENMARK DK

DESERTER rat

DESIRE yen

DETECTIVES CID, FBI, Feds, G-men, Yard

DI 501, Diana, Princess

DIAL face

DIAMONDS ice

DIANA Di

DIED d, ex, ob

DIMINUTIVE *indicates abbreviated form of name etc*

DIN noise, row

DINED ate, fed

DINNER din, meal

DIPLOMAT(S) ambassador, CD, Corps Diplomatique, HE

(DIRECT) CURRENT DC

DIRECTION bearing, N, S, E, W, NE, *etc*

DIS Hell, Underworld

DISC EP, LP, O

DISHEARTENED *indicates letter(s) removed from centre of word*

DISMISSED *any cricket dismissal*: b(owled), *etc*

DISPLAY air

DITTO do, same

DK Denmark

DO char, cheat, ditto, note, party, rook, same

DOCTOR Dr, GP, MB, MD, MO, vet

DOCTOR OF DIVINITY DD

DOCTRINE ism

DOG follow, tail, *any breed*: Alsatian, peke, *etc, any famous example*: Pluto, *etc*

DOM Dominican Republic, monk

DOMINICA WD

DOMINICAN REPUBLIC DOM

DON assume, Bradman, Spaniard

DOSSIER file

DOWN blue, low, *indicates reversal of letters in Down clue*

DR Doctor

DRACULA Count

DRINK tot, *any example*: ale, beer, gin, rum, *etc*

DRONE bee

DROP *indicates letter(s) deleted*

DRUG narcotic, *any example*: hash, hemp, grass, LSD, *etc*

DRY sec, TT

DU of the French

DUCK love, nought, O, *any example*: mallard, *etc*

DUKE D

DUTCH wife

DY Benin

DZ Algeria

E

E bearing, boat, bridge player, course, direction, East, ecstasy, energy, English, key, note, orient(al), partner, point, quarter, Spain

EA each, per, water

EACH ea, per

EAK Kenya

EARLY am

EARTH element

EAST E, bearing, course, direction, Orient, point, quarter

EASTERN oriental

EAT Tanzania

EAU Uganda

EC City, Ecuador

ECSTASY E

ECUADOR EC

ED edition, editor, Edward, (top) journalist

EDITION ed

EDITOR ed

EER always (poetic)

EG for example, for instance

EGG encourage, O, ovum, spur, urge

EGYPT ET

EIGHT crew, oarsmen

EIN, EINE a German

EL the Spanish, *indicates the letter* 'l'

ELEMENT air, earth, fire, water, *any chemical element*: C (carbon), Fe (iron), *etc*

ELEVEN (cricket) side, (football) team

ELI priest

ELITE AI (= A1), flower, pick

EL SALVADOR ES

ELY see

EM (printer's) measure, *indicates the letter* 'm'

EMBRACING *indicates letter(s) contained within a word*

EME uncle

EMPTY *indicates* 'O' *inserted*

EN (printer's) measure, *indicates the letter* 'n'

ENC enclosure

ENCLOSE fence, pen, *indicates letter(s) within a word*

ENCLOSURE enc, pen, pound, *indicates letter(s) within a word*

ENCOURAGE egg

END IN FRANCE fin

ENGINEER* CE, RE, sapper

ENGLISH E

ENTER log, record, *indicate(s) letters entering a word*

ENTOMB bury, inter, *indicates letter(s) buried within a word*

ENTRY *indicates letter(s) entering a word*

EP disc, epistle, (old) record

EPISTLE ep

ER Queen

ERA age, time

ERATO Muse

ERE before

ERGO so, therefore

ERIC fine

ERICA girl, heather, ling

EROS archer, bowman, Cupid

ERR* sin

ES El Salvador

EST Estonia

ESTIMATED TIME OF ARRIVAL ETA

ESTONIA EST

ET alien, and French, Egypt, extra-terrestrial

ETA arrival time, estimated time of arrival

ETH Ethiopia

ETHIOPIA ETH

EUTERPE Muse

EVEN evening (poetic)

EVENING even

EWE sheep

EX dead, died, former (husband, wife), from, late, once, out of, *indicating the letter* 'x'

EXCELLENCY ambassador, HE

EXCELLENT AI (= A1), first class

EXERCISE PE, PT, test

EXPERT ace, dab, master

EXPLORER *any example*: Cook, Polo, *etc*

EXPLOSIVE* HE, TNT

EXTRA b(ye), l(eg) b(ye), w(ide)

EXTRA LARGE OS, outsize

EXTRA-TERRESTRIAL ET

EYESORE stye

F

F fellow, folio, forte, France, key, loud, noisy, note

FA note, nothing

FACE dial, mug

FACTORY plant

FAIL plough

FAIRY peri

FAROE ISLANDS FR

FASHION* ton

FASHIONABLE in, U

FAST Lent

FATE Atropos, Clotho, Lachesis

FATHER churchman, clergyman, dad, Fr, Fra, generate, generator, pa, pop, sire

FBI detectives, feds, G-men

FE iron

FEDS detectives, FBI, G-men

FEET plates (Cockney)

FELLOW F, *indicates man's name*

FENCE enclosure, pale, receiver

FETE party

FEW *indicates Roman numerals up to ten*: I, II, IV, V, *etc*

FF folios, fortissimo, very loud

FIELDER *any position*: gully, mid-on, third man, *etc*

FIFTEEN side, team

FIFTY half ton, L

FIJI FJI

FILE dossier, line

FIN end in France, Finland

FINAL(LY) last, ult, ultimate, *indicates word-ending*

FINE eric

FINLAND FIN

FIRE element

FIREWORK banger

FIRST A, alpha, I (= 1), IST (= 1st), leading, top, winner, *indicates first letter(s) of word*

FIRST CLASS A, AI (= A1), ace, excellent

FISH angle, swimmer, *any example*: cod, dab, id, *etc*

FISHERMAN Peter

FJI Fiji

FL Liechtenstein

FLAG iris, jack, stone

FLAK AA, anti-aircraft

FLEET gaol, RN, Royal Navy, ships

FLIER airman, bird

FLIGHT OFFICER FO

FLOWER bloomer, pick, rill, river, stream *(plus any example)*, runner, *any example of flower*: arum, *etc*

FLYER airman, bird

FO airman, Flight Officer, folio

FOLIO(S) f, fo, ff

FOLLOW dog, tail

FORCE* *any services*: RAF, RN, *etc*

FORTE f, loud

FORTISSIMO ff, very loud

FORWARD hooker, prop, lock

FOUR boundary

FR dad, Faroe Islands, father, France

FRA brother, father, monk

FRANCE F, Fr

FREE* liberal

FRENCH Fr, *indicates French word*

FRENCHMAN M

FRENCHMEN MM

FRI Friday

FRIDAY F, Fri

FROM* ex, out of

FRONT van, *indicates beginning of word*

FURY Alecto, anger, ire, Megaera, Tisiphone

FUSS* ado

G

G girl, gramme, gravity, key, note

GA Georgia

GAL girl

GALLERY gods, Tate

GANGSTER Al (Capone)

GAOL clink, jug, stir, *any example*: Fleet, Reading, *etc*

GARDEN (OF ENGLAND) Kent

GB (Great) Britain

GBA Alderney (Channel Islands)

GBG Guernsey (Channel Islands)

GBJ Jersey (Channel Islands)

GBM Isle of Man
GBZ Gibraltar
GCA Guatemala
GE Georgia
GEN General, info, information, news
GENERAL Gen, *any example*: Grant, Lee, *etc*
GENERATE* father
GENERATOR dad, father
GENEROUS liberal
GEORGIA Ga, GE, girl
GERMAN *indicates German word*: das, der, die, Herr, Frau, *etc*
GERMANY D
GG horse
GH Ghana
GHANA GH
GI (American) soldier, Private
GIBRALTAR GBZ
GIRL deb, g, gal, miss, *any name*: Ann, Ella, Rose, *etc*
GK Greek
G-MAN agent, spy
G-MEN agents, spies
GO turn
GOAL score
GOAT butter
GOD/GODDESS *any example*: Ate, Isis, Mercury, Ra, *etc*
GODS gallery
GO FIRST lead, *indicates placement of letter(s) initially*
GO IN *indicates placement of letter(s) inside a word*
GOLD Au, or
GONE OFF away
GONG medal
GOOD MAN S, Saint, St
GP doctor, group, medical man
GR grain, gramme, Greece, Greek, King George
GRADUATE BA, MA, *etc*
GRAIN gr
GRAMME g, gr

GRAND K, M, piano, thousand
GRASS drug, inform, shop, sing, *any example*: bent, *etc*
GRAVE INSCRIPTION RIP
GRAVITY G
GREAT BRITAIN GB, UK
GREAT NUMBER host, *indicates large numeral*: C, D, M, *etc*
GREECE Gr
GREEK Gk, Gr
GREEK LETTER *any example*: beta, delta, mu, omega, pi, xi, *etc*
GREET cry, hail
GRENADA WG
GRILL* cook, question
GROUP* gp
GUARD SS
GUATEMALA GCA
GUERNSEY GBG
GUN banger
GUNNERS arsenal, RA
GUNS artillery
GUY Guyana
GUYANA GUY

H

H constant, hard, height, Henry, hospital, hot, hour, house, Hungary, hydrogen
HA Horse Artillery
HAIL ave, greet
HAIRSTYLE *any example*: bob, perm, *etc*
HAITI RH
HAL Harry, Henry
HALF TON fifty
HAM bacon, (poor) actor
HAND pass, worker
HANDS workers
HAPPY glad, jolly
HARBOUR port, *indicates letter(s) held within word or hidden word*

HARD h

HARD WATER ice

HARRY* Hal, Henry

HAS bears

HASH* drug

HAT cap, lid, *any example*: bowler, tile, *etc*

HE ambassador, helium, high explosive, His Eminence, (His) Excellency, man

HEAD ness, pate, point, *indicates start of word*

HEADLAND cape, ness

HEADQUARTERS HQ

HEAPS *indicates large numeral*: D, M, *etc*

HEAR(D) *indicates word(s) sound(s) like something else*

HEART *indicates middle of a word*

HEATHER erica, girl, ling

HEAVENLY BODY planet, sign of the zodiac, star, sun, *any examples*: Aries, Mars, Venus, Virgo, *etc*

HEED list

HEIGHT h

HELIUM He

HEMP drug, rope

HENRY H, Hal, Harry

HERMES Mercury

HERO DFC, DFM, DSC, DSM, GC, MC, VC

HG mercury

HIDE pelt, skin, *indicates hidden word, letter(s) inside word*

HIGH CLASS A, AI (= AI), U

HIGH EXPLOSIVE HE

HIGH SPEED TRAIN HST

HIGH TENSION HT

HILL tor

HIS EMINENCE HE

HIS/HER MAJESTY HM

HITCHED married, wed

HK Hong Kong

HKJ Jordan

HM Her/His Majesty, King, Queen

HO house

HOLD(S) *indicates letter(s) contained in a word*

HOLD(S) UP *indicates letters contained upside down*

HOLLAND linen

HOLY MAN S, Saint, St

HOLY TREE bo

HOME in

HOME COUNTIES SE

HOME HELP char, daily

HONG KONG HK

HONOUR *any example*: CH, OBE, OM, *etc*

HOOD archer, bowman

HOOKER forward

HORSE gg, mount, nag, *any breed*: arab, *etc*

HORSE ARTILLERY HA

HOSPITAL H

HOT h, stolen

HOUR h, hr

HOUSE cot, cottage, h, ho

HP never-never

HQ headquarters

HR Croatia, hour

HST high speed train

HT high tension

HUGE OS (outsize)

HUMOROUS CHARACTER card

HUNDRED C, century, land area, ton

HUNGARY H

HUSH sh

HYBRID* cross

HYDROGEN H

I

I a, ace, an, iodine, island, Italy, me, one (= 1), single

IAGO ancient

I AM Im (= I'm)

IAN Scot(sman), *indicates Scottish word*

IC in charge (of)

ICE diamonds, hard water, reserve

ICELAND IS

ID fish, I had/I would (=I'd), instinct, personality, self

IDA girl, mountain

IDE fish

IE that is, that's

IF an, provided

I HAD Id (= I'd)

II side, team (=11)

IL Illinois, Israel, the Italian

ILL* Illinois, I will (= I'll), illustrated

ILLINOIS Ill

ILLUSTRATED ill

IM I am (= I'm)

IMP (mischievous) child

IN (at) home, batting, fashionable, inch, Indiana, inside, not out, playing, *indicates letters within a word*

INCH in, island, move slowly

IN CHARGE (OF) ic, over

IN COURT up

IND India

INDEX list

INDIA IND

INDIANA IN

INDONESIA RI

INFO gen, information, news

INFORM grass, shop, sing

INFORMATION gen, info

IN FRONT *indicates letter(s) preceding*

INGE Dean

INITIAL(LY) *indicates first letter(s) of word(s)*

INN local, pub, tavern

INSECT *any example*: ant, bee, fly, gnat, tsetse, wasp, *etc*

INSIDE in, *indicates letter(s) within a word*

INST instant, this month

INSTANT inst

INSTINCT id

INSTRUMENT *any example*: oboe *(musical)*, scalpel *(medical)*

INTER between, bury, entomb, *indicates letter(s) between words*

INVEST besiege, *indicates letter(s) within a word*

IO joy, ten (10 = IO)

IODINE I

IOM (Isle of) Man

ION charge

IOU(S) debt(s)

IR Iran, iridium

IRAN IR

IRAQ IRQ

IRATE* cross

IRE anger, Ireland, rage

IRELAND composer, IRE, IRL

IRIDIUM Ir

IRIS flag

IRISHMAN Paddy, Pat

IRL Ireland

IRON club, Fe

IRQ Iraq

IS Iceland, island, (book of) Isaiah

IS ABLE can

ISAIAH Is

ISIS goddess, Thames

ISLAND ait, I, inch, Is, *any example*: Cos, IOM, Man, *etc*

ISLE (OF MAN) GBM, IOM

ISM theory

ISRAEL IL

ISSUE child

IST (= 1ST) alpha, first

IT Italian, SA, sex appeal, (the) thing, vermouth

ITALIAN It, vermouth, *indicates Italian word*

ITALY I

I WILL Ill (= I'll)
I WOULD Id (= (I'd)

J

J Jack, Japan, jay, judge, justice
JA Jamaica
JACK AB, flag, J, knave, lift, mariner, rating, sailor, tar
JAIL clink, jug
JAMAICA JA
JAPAN J, lacquer, varnish
JAPANESE oriental
JAY bird, *indicates the letter* 'j'
JE in Paris/France, I
JERSEY GBJ
JO little woman
JOCK Scot(sman), *indicates Scottish word*
JOG remind, trot
JOHN boy, loo
JOINT *any example*: ankle, baron, hip, knee, *etc*
JOLLY marine, RM
JORDAN HKJ
JOURNALIST ed
JOY girl, Io
JP Justice (of the Peace), magistrate
JUDGE beak, trier
JUG ewer, gaol, jail, prison
JUMPER *anything that jumps*: athlete, flea, *etc*
JUNCTION T
JUSTICE J, JP

K

K Cambodia, constant, grand, kay, Kelvin, kilo, king, knight, potassium, thousand
KAY girl, *indicates the letter* 'k'
KAZAKHSTAN KZ

KELVIN K
KENT SE, garden (of England)
KENTUCKY Ky
KENYA EAK
KEY A, B, C, D, E, F, G, central
KICK-OFF ko
KILO K
KIN relation, relative, *any example*: ma, pa, sis, *etc*
KINE cattle, oxen, neat
KING card, (chess)man, chess piece, HM, K, R, Rex, *any example*: George (GR), Lear, *etc*
KISS x
KM kilometre
KNAVE Jack
KNIGHT chess(man), chess piece, K, KT, N, sir
KNIGHT OF THE THISTLE KT
KNOCK OUT* ko
KO kick-off, knock out
KOREA (South) ROK
KS Kyrgyzstan
KT Knight (of the Thistle)
KUWAIT KWT
KWT Kuwait
KY Kentucky
KYRGYZSTAN KS
KZ Kazakhstan

L

L amateur, angle, apprentice, beginner, deb, lake, large, Latin, learner, left, length, Liberal, lira, loch, long, lots, lough, Luxembourg, novice, port, pound, pupil, scholar, side, student, tyro
LA Los Angeles, Louisiana, note, the French
LAB laboratory, Labour, politician, party
LABORATORY lab
LABOUR Lab, left, party

LACHESIS Fate

LACQUER Japan

LAD boy, *any (shortened) name*: Des, Phil, *etc*

LAIR den

LAKE L, *any example*: Erie, Victoria, *etc*

LAND AREA hundred

LANGUAGE tongue, *any example*: Erse, Latin, *etc*

LAO Laos

LAOS LAO

LAR Libya

LARGE L, OS

LARGE NUMBER *any larger Roman numeral*: C, D, L, M

LAST final, stay, *indicates last letter(s)*

LAST MONTH Dec, December, ult

LAST WORD amen

LAT Latin, latitude

LATE d, dead, ex

LATIN L, lat

LATITUDE lat

LATVIA LV

LB extra (leg bye), Liberia, measure, pound

LE the French

LEAD base metal, go first, Pb, van, *indicates first letter(s)*

LEADER(S) *indicates first letter(s)*

LEADING first, *indicates first letter(s)*

LEAN thin, list

LEARNER L, tyro

LEBANON RL

LEE General, river, shelter

LEFT Labour, port, side, sinister

LEG cricket side, limb, member, on

LEG BYE extra

LENGTH L, *any measurement*: ell, inch, *etc*

LES Leslie, the French

LESLIE Les

LESOTHO LS

LESS minus, *indicates letter(s) removed*

LETTUCE cos

LIB Liberal, politician, party

LIBERAL free, generous, L, Lib, politician, party

LIBERIA LB

LIBYA LAR

LID cap, hat, tile

LIE rest, story, tale

LIECHTENSTEIN FL

LIEUTENANT Lt

LIFT jack

LIGHT Very, window

LIMB arm, leg, member

LIMITED Ltd

LINCOLN (ABRAHAM) Abe

LINE file, railway, rank, row, tier

LINEN Holland

LINES BR, ode, poem, rly, ry, verse

LINESMAN poet

LING erica, fish, heather

LIONEL Bart

LIRA L

LIST heed, index, lean, listen, table

LITHUANIA LT

LITTLE *indicates abbreviation*

LITTLE WOMAN Jo

LO look, see

LOAD(S) *indicates large number*: C, D, M, *etc*

LOCAL inn, pub, tavern

LOCALITY *any district*: EC, NE, *etc*

LOCH L, lough, *any example*: Ness, *etc*

LOCK forward, tress

LOG enter, logarithm, record

LOGARITHM log

LONG l, pine

LOO John

LOOK lo, see

LOOT spoils, swag

LOS ANGELES LA

LOT(S) many, *indicates large number*: C, D, M, *etc*

LOUD f, forte

LOUGH L, loch, *any example*: Erne, *etc*

LOUISIANA La

LOVE cupid, duck, nothing, nought, O

LOW blue, cartoonist, down, moo, sad

LOWER cow

LP disc, record

LS Lesotho

LSD drug, old money

LT Lieutenant, Lithuania

LTD limited

LUXEMBOURG L

LV Latvia

M

M em, Frenchman, grand, great number, maiden, male, Malta, man, many, mark, married, masculine, mass, master, member, meridiem, metre, midday, mile, Monday, monsieur, motorway, noon, thousand

MA graduate, Massachusetts, Master of Arts, Morocco, mother, mum, scholar

MAC Scot(sman), *indicates Scottish word*

MACEDONIA MK

MAD* crazy

MADAGASCAR RM

MADAME Mme

MADEMOISELLE Mlle

MAG bird, magazine

MAGISTRATE beak, JP

MAGNESIUM Mg

MAIDEN m, miss

MAIN sea

MAINE Me

MAIN FORCE navy, RN

MAKE FAST moor

MAL Malaysia

MALAWI MW

MALAYSIA MAL

MALE m, masculine

MALI RMM

MALLARD duck

MALTA M

MAN chess piece, he, Island, Isle, m, male, sailor, soldier

MANAGING DIRECTOR MD

MANGANESE Mn

MANUSCRIPT ms

MANY *indicates large number*: C, D, M, *etc*

MAR* March, married

MARCH Mar

MARCH PAST April

MARINE jolly, RM

MARINER AB, Jack

MARK boy, m

MARRIED hitched, m, mar, spliced, wed

MARYLAND Md

MASCULINE m, male

MASS M, Massachusetts, service

MASSACHUSETTS Ma, Mass

MASTER ace, beak, captain, dab, expert, M, MA, painter, skipper, tutor

MASTER OF ARTS MA

MASTER OF CEREMONIES MC

MATE ally

MATERIAL *any example*: drill, net, rep, *etc*

MAURITANIA RIM

MAURITIUS MS

MAYBE* say

MAYFAIR West End, WI (= W1)

MB Bachelor of Medicine, doctor

MBE decoration

MC decoration, Master of Ceremonies, medal, Military Cross, Monaco

MD Doctor (of Medicine), Managing Director, Maryland, Musical Director

ME I (object), Maine, Middle East, Middle English, note

MEASURE dance, tot, *any (abbreviated) example*: centimetre, ell, em, en, foot, inch, kilometre, ounce, perch, pole, rod, yard, *etc*

MEDAL gong, *any example*: MBE, MC

MEDICAL MAN Dr, GP, *etc*

MEGAERA Fury

MELPOMENE Muse

MEMBER arm, leg, limb, M, MP

MERCURY Hermes, Hg, quicksilver

MERCY quarter

MERIDIEM m, midday, N, noon

METRE m

MEX Mexico

MEXICO MEX

MG car, magnesium

MI motorway (= M1), note

MIDDAY m, meridiem, n, noon

MIDDLE EAST/ENGLISH ME

MIEN air

MILE m

MILITARY CROSS MC

MILITARY MEDAL MM

MILITARY POLICE MP, redcap

MILL philosopher

MILLIMETRE mm

MINUS less, *indicates omission of letter(s)*

MISS girl, maiden, Mississippi

MISSING *indicates omission of letter(s)*

MISSISSIPPI Miss

MISSOURI Mo

MISTER Mr

MISTRESS Mrs

MK Macedonia

MLLE French girl, Mademoiselle

MM Frenchmen, Military Medal, millimetre

MME Madame

MN manganese

MO doctor, Missouri, moment, second

MOMENT mo, second

MON Monday, Scotsman

MONACO MC

MONDAY M, Mon

MONEY brass, cash, LSD, p, penny, *any example*: cents, dollars, pounds, *etc*

MONK brother, Dom, Fra, member of order, *any example*: Dominican, *etc*

MONSIEUR M

MONTH *any (abbreviated) example*: Jan, Feb, Mar, *etc*

MOO low

MOOR make fast, Othello

MORNING am

MOROCCO MA

MOTHER dam, ma, mum, *etc*

MOTORWAY M, MI (= M1)

MOUNT horse, gg, mountain, mt, *indicates letter(s) on top*

MOUNTAIN(S) mt, mount, range, *any example*: Alps, Ida, *etc*

MOVE SLOWLY inch

MP Member (of Parliament), Military/Mounted Police, politician, redcap, representative

MR mister

MRS mistress, wife

MS manuscript, Mauritius, (hand)writing

MU Greek character

MUG face, rob

MUM ma, mother, quiet

MURPHY potato, spud

MUSE(S) Calliope, Clio, Erato,

Euterpe, Melpomene, Polyhymnia, Terpsichore, Thalia, Urania

MUSEUM BM

MUSIC *any notes*: A, B, C, Do(h), Re, Me, breve, quaver, *etc, any form*: classical, rock, *etc*

MUSICAL *any example*: Evita, Hair, *etc*

MUSICAL DIRECTOR MD

MUSICIAN player, *any example*: oboist, pianist, *etc*

MUSKETEER(S) Aramis, Athos, Porthos

MW Malawi

MYANMAR (BURMA) BUR

N

N bearing, bridge player, course, direction, en, knight, meridiem, midday, name, neuter, new, nitrogen, noon, north, Norway, noun, partner (bridge), point, pole, quarter

NA Netherlands Antilles, sodium

NAG horse

NAM Namibia

NAME n

NAMIBIA NAM

NAT born

NATIONAL TRUST NT

NAVY main force, RN

NB (take) note

NCO Cpl, non-commissioned officer, RSM, Sergeant, Sgt

ND no date

NE bearing, born, north-east, Tyneside, quarter

NEAT cattle, cow, kine, ox(en)

NECK col

NEE born

NEGATIVE no

NESS head(land), point

NETHERLANDS NL

NETHERLANDS ANTILLES NA

NEUTER n

NEVER-NEVER HP

NEW* n

NEWS gen, info

NEWSPAPER daily, *any example*: *Express, Times, etc*

NEW TESTAMENT NT

NEW YORK city, NY

NEW ZEALAND NZ

NI nickel, Northern Ireland

NIB writer

NIC Nicaragua

NICARAGUA NIC

NICE resort

NICKEL Ni, coin

NIGER RN

NIGERIA WAN

NIL no, nothing, nought, O, zero

NITROGEN N

NL Netherlands

NO negative, nil, not out, number, O

NO DATE nd

NOISE din, row, *indicates sounds like*

NOISY f, forte

NON-COMMISSIONED OFFICER Corporal, Cpl, NCO

NON-DRINKER TT

NON-DRINKERS AA, abstainers

NOON m, meridiem, midday, n

NOR Norway

NORTH bearing, direction, N, point, pole, quarter

NORTH-EAST NE

NORTHERN IRELAND NI

NORTH-WEST NW

NORWAY N, Nor

NOSE beak

NOTE nb, *any musical example*: A, B, C, D, E, F, G, Do(h), Re, Me/Mi, Fa(h), So(h), Sol, La(h), Te/Ti; breve, crotchet, *etc, any paper money*: fiver, *etc*

NOTES currency, music

NOTHING FA, love, nil, nought, O, zero

NOTICE ad

NOT OUT at home, batting, in, no

NOUGHT duck, love, nil, nothing, O, zero

NOUN n

NOVEL *any example*: *Middlemarch, She, etc*

NOVELIST writer, *any example*: Lear, Poe, *etc*

NOVICE L

NOWADAYS ad, present

NT bible, books, National Trust, New Testament, preservationists

NUMBER anaesthetic, no, tell, *any example*: I, II, III; ein, one, un(e), *etc*

NUN member of order, sister, *any example*: Cistercian, *etc*

NUR railwaymen

NURSE sister, tend

NUT teachers

NW bearing, direction, north-west, quarter

NY New York

NYM Corporal

NZ New Zealand

O

O ball, circle, circuit, disc, duck, egg, love, nil, no, nothing, nought, Oh, Ohio, ought, oxygen, ring, round, zero

OAP pensioner, senior citizen

OAR row, scull

OARSMEN crew, eight

OB died, obit, Old Boy

OBIT ob

OBOIST airman

OCCUPATIONAL THERAPY OT

ODD* uneven, *indicates odd letters*

ODDS SP

ODE lines, poem

OE Old English

OFF cricket side

OFFICER *any example*: Adm, Brig, Cap, Capt, CO, Col, *etc*

OFFSPRING issue

OF THE FRENCH de, de la, des, du

OH O, Ohio

OHIO O, Oh

OK all right

OLD(EN) ancient, once, *indicates old usage*

OLD BOY OB

OLD CITY Ur

OLD ENGLISH OE

OLD TESTAMENT OT

ON* about, concerning, cricket side, leg, playing, *indicates letter(s) above/below*

ON BOARD aboard, afloat, *indicates letters between* 'SS'

ONCE ex, old

ONE a, ace, an, I (= 1)

ONE COMING OUT deb, debutante

ON HORSEBACK up

OP operation, opus, work

OPERATION op

OPUS Op

OR alternative(ly), gold

ORCHESTRA musicians, players

ORDER* *any example of honour*: OBE, OM, *etc*

ORDINARY SEAMAN OS

ORGAN *any example*: heart, *etc*

ORIENT E, East

ORIENT(AL) Chinese, East, Eastern, Japanese

OS AB, extra large, huge, Ordinary Seaman, outsize, sailor, tar

OT bible, books, Old Testament, occupational therapy

OTHELLO Moor

OTHERS rest

OUGHT O

OUNCE cat, measure, oz

OUT* blooming

OUT OF ex, from

OUTSIZE OS

OVER concerning, dead, in charge (of), re, six balls/deliveries, *indicates letter(s) above*

OVERTURN(ED)* spill, upset, *indicates letters reading backwards in Down clue*

OVUM egg

OX neat

OXEN cattle, kine, neat

OXFORD shoe

OXYGEN O

OZ Australia, ounce

P

P copper, money, page, parking, pawn, penny, phosphorus, piano, Portugal, power, president, quiet, soft(ly)

PA dad, Panama, Pennsylvania, Philadelphia, pop, sire

PADDY Irishman

PAGE(S) p, pp

PAINTER artist, master, rope, RA, *any example*: Titian, *etc*

PAINTING art

PAIR pr

PAKISTAN PK

PAL ally

PALE ashen, fence

PANAMA PA

PAPERBACK pb

PAPUA NEW GUINEA PNG

PARAGUAY PY

PARCEL *indicates letters within a word*

PARISIAN *indicates French word*

PARKING P

PART *indicates hidden word or part of word*

PARTNER N, S, E, W (bridge)

PARTY do, fete, *any example*: Con(servative), Lab(our), Lib(eral), Tory, *etc*

PAS dance, step

PASS col, hand

PAT Irishman

PATE head, starter

PAWN chess piece, man, P, pledge, pop

PAWNBROKER uncle

PB lead, paperback

PC bobby, copper, peeler, policeman, postcard

PE exercises, Peru, physical education, PT

PECKER beak

PED pedestrian

PEDESTRIAN ped

PEELER copper, PC, policeman

PEG tee

PELT hide, skin

PEN author, enclosure, prison, swan, writer, *indicates letter(s) within a word*

PENCIL writer

PENNSYLVANIA Pa

PENNY coin, copper, d, girl's name, money, p

PENSIONER OAP, senior citizen

PER a, ea, (for) each

PERCH fish, measure, pole, rod, roost

PERHAPS* say

PERI fairy

PERM hairstyle

PERSONALITY id

PERSON WHO HESITATES butter

PERU PE

PETER fisherman, safe

PHIL (small) boy, man, Philadelphia, Philharmonic, philosophy

PHILADELPHIA Pa

PHILANTHROPIST Tate

PHILHARMONIC Phil

PHILIPPINES RP

PHILOSOPHER *any example*: Mill, Plato, *etc*

PHILOSOPHY phil

PHONE blower

PHOSPHORUS P

PHYSICAL EDUCATION/EXERCISE/TRAINING PE, PT

PI Greek letter, pious, religious

PIANISSIMO pp, very soft(ly)

PIANIST musician

PIANO grand, instrument, p, soft(ly)

PICK elite, flower

PIECE man, *any chess piece*: pawn, rook, *etc*

PILOT OFFICER PO

PINE long, tree

PIOUS pi

PK Pakistan

PL Poland

PLA River (Port of London) Authority

PLANET heavenly body, *any example*: Mars, *etc*

PLANT factory, *any example*: climber, daff, pink, *etc*

PLATES (*Cockney*) feet

PLAY bow

PLAYER actor, musician, record, thespian, *any example*: Gielgud, *etc*

PLAYERS cast, musicians, orchestra, records, side, team, XI, XV

PLAYING* in, on

PLEDGE pawn, pop

PLO terrorists

PLOUGH fail

PM afternoon, post meridiem, post mortem, Prime Minister

PNG Papua New Guinea

POEM lines, ode

POET linesman, *indicates poetic form of word, any example*: anon, Keats, Shelley, *etc*

POETIC(ALLY) *indicates poetic form of word*

POETRY lines

POINT N(orth), S(outh), E(ast), W(est), fielder, head, ness

POLAND PL

POLE N(orth), S(outh), perch

POLICEMAN PC, peeler

POLITICIAN Con(servative), Lab(our), Lib(eral), MP, Republican, Tory

POLYHYMNIA Muse

POOR ACTOR ham

POP dad, father, pa, pawn, sire

PORT bearing, harbour, L, left, *any example*: Dover, Rio, *etc*

PORTHOS Musketeer

PORTUGAL P

POSTCARD pc

POSTER ad

POST MERIDIEM afternoon, pm

POST MORTEM PM

POSTSCRIPT afterthought, PPS, PS, *indicates letter(s) added*

POTASSIUM K

POTATO murphy

POUND enclosure, l, lb

POWER P

PP pages, pianissimo, very soft

PPS addition, afterthought, postscript, second thoughts, *indicates letter(s) added*

PR pair, price, priest, public relations

PRES president

PRESENT (TIME) AD, Christmas

PRESERVATIONISTS NT

PRESERVE can

PRESIDENT P, Pres

PRICE pr

PRIEST p, pr, *any example*: Eli, *etc*

117

PRIESTS clergy, cloth

PRIME MINISTER PM

PRINCE(SS) *any example*: Di, Diana, Harry, *etc*

PRINTER'S MEASURE em, en

PRISON brig, jug, pen, stir, *any example*: Fleet, Reading, *etc*

PRIVATE GI

PRO Public Relations Officer

PROLIFIC POET anon

PRONOUN *any example*: I, me, my, he, his, her, *etc*

PROP forward

PROPHET *any example*: Amos, Isaiah, *etc*

PROPPING UP *indicates letters supported in Down clue*

PROVIDED if

PS addition, afterthought, post-script, second thoughts, *indicates letter(s) added*

PT (physical) training

PUB(LIC HOUSE) inn, local, tavern

PUBLIC RELATIONS (OFFICER) PR(O)

PUMP question, shoe

PUPIL L

PUT IN *indicates letter(s) inserted*

PY Paraguay

Q

Q Quebec, queen, question

QC silk

QUA as

QUARTER mercy, *any example*: N, S, E, W, NE, SW, *etc*

QUEBEC Q

QUEEN chess piece, ER, HM, Q, R, Regina, *any example*: Anne, Victoria, *etc*

QUESTION pump, q

QUICKSILVER mercury

QUIET(LY) mum, p

R

R castle, king, queen, radius, recipe, regina, resistance, rex, right, river, road, rook, run(s), side, starboard, take

RA Argentina, arsenal, artillery, artist, god, gunners, painter, radium

RACE TT

RADICAL root

RADIUM Ra

RADIUS r

RAF (Royal Air) Force

RAGE* anger, ire

RAILWAY BR, line, rly, ry, *any example*: GNER, GWR, SR, Virgin, *etc*

RAILWAYMEN NUR

RAISE rear, *indicates letters reversed in Down clue*

RAM Aries, butter

RANGE mountains, *any example*: Alps, Andes, Urals, *etc*

RANK line, tier

RATE mph, speed

RATING AB, Jack, sailor, tar

RAY fish

RB Botswana

RC Roman Catholic, Taiwan

RCA Central African Republic

RCB Congo

RCH Chile

RD road

RE about, note, over, Religious Education, Royal Engineers, sapper(s), soldier(s)

REBEL* revolt, revolutionary, *any example*: Cade, Straw, Tyler, *etc*

REBELLING revolting

RECEIVER fence

RECIPE* r, take

RECORD enter, EP, log, LP

REDCAP Military Policeman, MP

REGIMENTAL SERGEANT MAJOR RSM

REGINA Q(ueen), R

RELATION(S) kin, tale, *any example*: aunt, bro, dad, *etc*

RELATIVE(S) kin, *any example*: ma, pa, sis, *etc*

RELIGIOUS pi

RELIGIOUS EDUCATION RE

RELIGIOUS INSTRUCTION RI

REMIND jog

REP repertory, representative, republican, salesman

REPERTORY rep

REPRESENTATIVE agent, MP, rep, salesman, traveller

REPUBLICAN politician, rep

RES (Latin) thing

RESERVE ice

RESISTANCE R

RESORT* spa, *any example*: Bath, Nice, *etc*

REST bridge, lie, others

RESTING *indicates letter(s) in* 'bed' *or* 'cot'

RET soak

RETIRE(D) *indicates letters reversed; indicates letters in* 'bed' *or* 'cot'

RETREAT den, *indicates letters reversed*

REV(D) vicar

REVOLT* rebel, revolution

REVOLTING* rebelling

REVOLUTION* revolt

REVOLUTIONARY* Che, rebel

REX boy, king, R

RH Haiti

RHODE ISLAND RI

RI Indonesia, Religious Instruction, Rhode Island

RIB wife

RIGHT r, rt, side, starboard, Tories

RILL brook, flower, runner, stream

RIM Mauritania

RING circle, O

RIP* grave inscription, rest in peace, tear

RIVER flower, R, *any example*: Dee, Exe, Po, *etc*

RIVER AUTHORITY PLA

RL Lebanon

RLY lines, railway

RM jolly, Madagascar, (Royal) Marine

RMM Mali

RN fleet, (main) force, Niger, Royal Navy

RO Romania

ROAD avenue, r, rd, st, street, way

ROB boy's name, mug

ROCK *any example*: granite, *etc*

ROD pole, perch, staff

ROK Korea, Republic of (South Korea)

ROLLS-ROYCE RR

ROMANIA RO

ROOK castle, chess piece, do, R

ROOST perch

ROOT radical

ROPE hemp, painter

ROU Uruguay

ROUND O, *indicates letter(s) around/within word*

ROW* line, oar, scull, tier

ROYAL ENGINEER(S) RE, sapper(s)

ROYAL MARINE(S) RM

ROYAL NAVY fleet, force, RN

RP Philippines

RR bishop, Rolls-Royce

RSM NCO, Regimental Sergeant Major, San Marino

RT right

RU Burundi, Rugby Union

RUGBY (UNION) RU

RULER *any example*: Ivan, Victoria, *etc*

RUN(S) r

RUNNER flower, R, river

RUS Russia

RUSSIA RUS

RV bible

RWA Rwanda

RWANDA RWA

RY lines, railway

S

S bearing, bob, bridge player, course, direction, holy man, partner, pole, quarter, Sabbath, saint, Saturday, second, shilling, small, son, South(ern), sulphur, sun, Sunday, Sweden

SA army, it, sex appeal

SABBATH S

SABLE black

SACK sherry

SAD low

SAFE peter

SAILOR AB, Jack, man, OS, rating, salt, tar

SAINT good man, holy man, S, St

SAINTS SS

SALESMAN rep, representative, traveller

SALT sailor

SAME do (ditto)

SAMOA WS

SAN MARINO RSM

SAPPER(S) engineer(s), RE, Royal Engineer(s)

SAT Saturday

SATURDAY S, Sat

SAUSAGE banger

SAY maybe, perhaps

SC science

SCH school

SCHOLAR BA, L, MA

SCHOOL sch, *any example*: Eton, Harrow, *etc*

SCIENCE sc

SCIENTIST BSc, *any example*: Bacon, Darwin, *etc*

SCOLD nag

SCORE twenty, *any example*: goal, try, *etc*

SCOT tax, *any name of Scotsman*: Ian, Jock, Mac, *etc*

SCOTSMAN mon, *any name of Scotsman*: Bruce, Sandy, *etc*

SCOTTISH *indicates Scottish word/ pronunciation*

SCOTTISH FLOWERS burns

SCULL oar, row

SD Swaziland

SE bearing, direction, Home Counties, Kent, quarter, south-east

SEA deep, main, *any example*: Dead, North, *etc*

SEAMAN AB

SEASON salt, time, *any example*: autumn, spring, *etc*

SEC dry, second, secretary

SECOND mo, s, sec

SECOND-HAND sh

SECOND THOUGHTS ps, pps

SECRETARY sec

SEE lo, look, v, vide, *any example*: Ely, Rome, *etc*

SENEGAL SN

SENIOR CITIZEN OAP

SENOR Spaniard, Sr

SENTENCE stretch, time

SERGE cloth

SERPENT (musical) instrument, *any example*: asp, python, *etc*

SERVICE ace, mass, *any example*: army, air force, navy, RAF, RN, *etc*

SEX APPEAL it, SA

SEYCHELLES SY

SGP Singapore

SH hush, quiet, second-hand

SHADE spirit

SHAKESPEARE Bard, Will

SHE *(title of)* novel, woman

SHEEP ewe, ram, teg, tup
SHELTER lee
SHERRY sack
SHILLING s
SHIP boat, SS, vessel, *any example*: brig, cruiser, ketch, liner, sloop, *etc*
SHIPS fleet, navy
SHOE Oxford, pump, *etc*
SHOP grass, inform, sing
SHORTLY anon, *indicates shortened form*
SIDE fifteen, l(eft), players, r(ight), XI, XV
SIERRA LEONE WAL
SILK QC
SILVER Ag
SIN err, *any example*: gluttony, sloth, *etc*
SING grass, inform, shop
SINGAPORE SGP
SINGER *any example*: alto, baritone, bass, soprano, tenor, *etc*
SINGLE I (= 1)
SINISTER left
SIR knight
SIRE father, pa, pop
SIR PETER Brook
SIS sister
SISTER nun, nurse, sis
SIX boundary
SIX BALLS deliveries, over
SIXTH FORM upper class
SK Slovakia
SKIN hide, pelt
SKIPPER Capt, captain, master
SLO Slovenia
SLOTH ai
SLOVAKIA SK
SLOVENIA SLO
SMALL s, *indicates diminutive, shortened version, particularly names, states*
SME Surinam(e)
SN Senegal

SNAGGED caught, trapped, *indicates letter(s) within a word*
SNAKE *any example*: adder, viper, *etc*
SO ergo, such, therefore, thus
SOAK ret
SOCIALLY ACCEPTABLE U
SOCIAL WORKER ant
SODIUM Na
SOFT(LY) p, piano
SOL note, sun
SOLDIER man, RE
SOLDIERS army, REs, TA, *etc*
SOME *indicates hidden word, part of word*
SON s
SOON anon
SOUND *indicates sounds like*
SOUTH bearing, direction, point, pole, quarter, S
SOUTH AFRICA ZA
SOUTH-EAST SE
SOUTH-WEST SW
SP betting, odds, starting price
SPA resort, spring
SPAIN E
SPANIARD Don, Senor, Sr
SPANISH *indicates Spanish word*
SPANNER arch, bridge
SPEAK *indicates sounds like*
SPEED drug, mph, rate
SPIES CIA
SPILL* overturn, upset
SPIRIT shade, *any example*: gin, rum, vodka, *etc*
SPLICED married, wed
SPOIL(S)* loot, mar(s), swag
SPRING season, spa
SPUD murphy
SPUR egg
SQUARE T
SR Senor, Spaniard
SRI LANKA CL

SS boat, bodyguard, guard, on board *(indicates letters in between)*, saints, vessel

ST good man, holy man, road, saint, stone, street, way

STAFF rod, workers

STAR heavenly body, *any example*: Sirius, sun, *etc*

STARBOARD r, right

STARTER *any example*: pâté, *etc*, *indicates first letter of a word*

STATE *any example, particularly abbreviated US*: Ala, Cal, Ga, Mass, *etc*

STARTING PRICE SP

STAY last

STEP pas

STIR* gaol, jail, mix, prison

ST LUCIA WL

STOLEN hot

STONE flag, st, *any example*: diamond, granite, *etc*

STORY account, lie, tale

STREAM brook, flower, rill

STREET road, st, way

STRETCH sentence, time (in prison)

STUDENT L

STUDY con, den

ST VINCENT AND THE GRENADINES WV

STYE eyesore

SU Belarus

SUB below, U-boat, under

SUCH so

SULPHUR S

SUN S, sol, Sunday

SUNDAY S, Sun

SUPPORT bra, *indicates letter(s) below in Down clue*

SURINAM(E) SME

SW bearing, direction, quarter, south-west

SWAG loot, spoils

SWALLOW bird, *indicates letter(s) enclosed*

SWAN cob, pen

SWAZILAND SD

SWEDEN S

SWIMMER fish, *any example of creature that swims*: eel, otter, *etc*

SWITZERLAND CH

SY Seychelles

SYR Syria

SYRIA SYR

T

T junction, square, tee, time, ton, Tuesday

TA soldiers, (Territorial) Army, thanks

TABLE board, list

TAIWAN RC

TAJIKISTAN TJ

TAKE r, recipe

TAKE IN *indicates letter(s) enclosed by word*

TAKE ON *indicates letter(s) joined on to word*

TAKE UP *indicates letter(s) introduced backwards into word*

TALE account, lie, story

TAR AB, Jack, OS, rating, sailor

TATE gallery, philanthropist

TAU cross

TAVERN inn, local, pub

TAX scot

TEA cha, char

TEACHER beak

TEACHERS NUT

TEAM eleven, II (= 11), fifteen, XI, XV, players, *any example*: Arsenal, Villa, *etc*

TEE peg, *indicates the letter* 't'

TEETOTAL TT

TEETOTALLERS abstainers

TEG sheep

TELL archer, bowman, number

TEN IO (= 10)
TEND nurse
TERPSICHORE Muse
TERRITORIAL ARMY TA
TERRORISTS IRA, PLO
TEST exercise
TG Togo
TH Thursday
THAILAND T
THALIA Muse
THAMES flower, Isis
THANKS ta
THAT IS ie
THE (definite) article
THE FRENCH le, la, les
THE GAMBIA WAG
THE GERMAN das, der, die
THE ITALIAN il *(usually)*
THEORY ism
THE PRESENT AD
THEREFORE ergo, so
THE SPANISH el *(usually)*
THESPIAN actor, player
THIN lean
THING res (Latin), it
THIS MONTH inst
THOUSAND grand, K, M
THURS Thursday
THURSDAY Th, Thurs
THUS so
TI titanium
TIER line, rank, row
TILE hat
TIME season, sentence, stretch, t, *any example*: hour, min(ute), sec(ond), *etc*
TIMES daily
TIN can, cash
TIRO beginner
TISIPHONE Fury
TITANIUM Ti
TITLE *any peer*: lady, lord, *etc*
TJ Tajikistan

TM Turkmenistan
TO AND FRO *indicates a palindrome*
TOGO TG
TOLERATE brook
TON C, century, fashion, hundred, t
TONGUE language, *any example*: French, German, *etc*
TOOL *any example*: axe, spanner, wrench, *etc*
TOP ace, *indicates first letter(s)*
TOR hill
TORIES right
TORT wrong
TORY blue, C, Con(servative), party, politician
TOT child, drink, measure
TO THE FRENCH a la, au
TR Turkey
TRAINING PT
TRAINS BR
TRANSLATOR tr
TRANSPORT *any example*: BA, BR, bus, cab, car, ry, taxi, train, van, *etc*
TRAP *indicates letter(s) caught within word*
TRAP(PED) snag(ged), *indicates letter(s) caught within word*
TRAVELLER rep, representative, salesman
TRESS lock
TRIER judge
TRINIDAD AND TOBAGO TT
TROT jog
TRUMPETER airman
TRY score
TT dry, (bike) race, non-drinker, teetotal, Trinidad and Tobago
TTS abstainers
TUC workers
TUESDAY T, Tues
TUNE air
TUNISIA TN

TUP ram, sheep
TURKEY TR
TURKMENISTAN TM
TURN* corner, go, U, *indicates letters reversed*
TUTOR master
TWENTY score
TYNESIDE NE
TYRO amateur, beginner, L, learner

UR old city
URANIA Muse
URANIUM U
URGE egg
URN vessel
URUGUAY ROU
US America(n), useless
USA America
USELESS US

U

U acceptable, all right, boat, fashionable, (socially) acceptable, turn, universal, university, upper class, uranium, Uruguay
UA Ukraine
U-BOAT sub
UK United Kingdom
UKRAINE UA
ULT final, last month, ultimate
ULTIMATE final, ult
UN a French
UNCLE Bob, eme, pawnbroker
UNCLE SAM America, USA
UNDER sub, *indicates letter(s) below*
UNE a French
UNEVEN* odd, *indicates odd letters*
UNION *any example*: NUR, *etc*
UNITED KINGDOM UK
UNITED NATIONS UN
UNITED STATES (OF AMERICA) US(A)
UNIVERSAL general, U
UNIVERSITY U
UNKNOWN x, y
UP at university, in court, on horseback, *indicates letter(s) reading upwards*
UPPER CLASS sixth form, U
UPSET* overturn, spill, *indicates letters reversed*

V

V against, anti, see, vanadium, Vatican (City), versus, velocity, very, vide, victory, volt, vol(ume), vs
VA Virginia
VALEDICTION bye
VAN front, vehicle
VANADIUM V
VARNISH Japan
VATICAN (CITY) V
VEHICLE *any example*
VELOCITY v
VENEZUELA YV
VERMOUTH It, Italian
VERSE lines, ode, poetry, v
VERSUS against, anti, v, vs
VERY light, v
VERY LOUD(LY)/NOIS(IL)Y ff, fortissimo
VERY SOFT(LY) pp, pianissimo
VESSEL boat, can, SS, urn, *any example*: brig, ketch, *etc*
VET doctor
VICAR Rev(d)
VICTORY V
VIDE see, V
VIETNAM VN
VIOLINIST bowman
VIRGINIA Va
VN Vietnam
VOL book, v, volume

VOLKSWAGEN Beetle, VW
VOLT v
VOLUME book, v, vol
VOTE x
VS against, anti, V, versus
VW Beetle, Volkswagen

W

W bearing, bridge player, course, direction, extra (cricket), partner, point, quarter, watt, Wednesday, West(ern), wide, wife, women
WAG The Gambia
WAL Sierra Leone
WAN ashen, pale, Nigeria
WATER Aq, ea, element
WATT W
WAY av(enue), ave, st(reet)
WD Dominica
WEAPON *any example*: bomb, gun, sword, *etc*
WEAPONS artillery
WED hitched, married, spliced, we would (= we'd), Wednesday
WEDNESDAY W, Wed
WEIGHT *any example*: dram, gram, lb, ounce, oz, pound, *etc*
WELCOME* ave
WELSH *indicates Welsh name, county, river, town*: Owen, Glam(organ), Usk, Swansea, *etc*
WELSHMAN Dai, Evans, Jones, Lewis, Taff, *etc*
WEST bearing, direction, point, quarter, W
WEST END Mayfair, WI (= W1)
WEST INDIES WI
WE WOULD wed (= we'd)
WG Grenada
WHY *sounds like* 'y'
WI Mayfair (W1), West End (W1), West Indies
WIDE extra, w

WIFE Dutch, Mrs, rib, ux(or)
WILD* mad
WILL Bill, Shakespeare
WINDOW light
WINE *any example*: Claret, Graves, Hock, *etc*
WINGER bird
WITH *indicates letter(s) adjoining*
WITHIN *indicates letter(s) inside*
WITH ITALIAN con
WL St Lucia
WOMAN she, *any name*: Ada, Eve, *etc*
WOMEN w
WORK* op
WORKER ant, bee, hand
WORKERS hands, staff, TUC
WRITER novelist, pen, nib, pencil, *any example*: Bacon, Bronte, Chaucer, *etc*
WRONG* tort, X
WS Samoa
WV St Vincent and the Grenadines

X

X chromosome, cross, ex, kiss, unknown, vote, wrong
XI players, (cricket) side
XV players, side

Y

Y chromosome, unknown, yard, year, yen, yttrium
YANK(EE) American
YARD y
YEAR y, yr
YEMEN ADN
YEN Y

YR year
YTTRIUM Y
YU Yugoslavia
YUGOSLAVIA YU
YV Venezuela

Z

Z Zambia, zed, zero
ZA South Africa
ZAMBIA Z

ZED *indicates letter* 'z'
ZERO nil, nothing, nought, O (= 0), z
ZIMBABWE ZW
ZINC Zn
ZIRCONIUM Zr
ZN zinc
ZO cross
ZR zirconium
ZRE Democratic Republic of Congo
ZW Zimbabwe

Roman Numerals

I one
II two
III three
IV four
V five
VI six
VII seven
VIII eight
IX nine
X ten
XI eleven
XV fifteen

XVI sixteen
L fifty
LI fifty-one
C one hundred
CL one hundred and fifty
CC two hundred
D five hundred
DI five hundred and one
M one thousand
MD fifteen hundred
MM two thousand

Help for Graded Puzzles

This section is designed to act as a buffer zone between the puzzles and solutions. It can be used for reference both when you are stuck on a particular clue and when you have got a solution but don't understand how it is constructed or why it is correct.

Various conventions detailed below have been followed when explicating the clue devices.

Roman type indicates words that are directly quoted from clues.
UPPER CASE letters are employed for elements of the solutions.
Italicized type is used to give a plain English paraphrase of the instructional elements within a clue.
'Single quotes' appear round words or phrases that are a prerequisite to a final solution but not the solution itself.

Clue types [a] and [b] are glossed by *Double definition* and *Single definition* respectively because it is rarely easy to explain such clues without giving the solution — which we have tried to avoid doing here. In certain cases, however, we have included an explanation within square brackets of any clues that depend on a rather athletic leap of the imagination.

PUZZLE 1

ACROSS

4 Second = S + coach = trainer **8** *Double definition* **9** cut down = REAP + fruit = PEAR **10** Period of time = AGE *after* brief = SHORT **11** *Double definition* **12** *Anagram*: machine + call initially = C **13** *Single definition* **16** demonstration = SHOW + defeated = DOWN **19** *Single definition* **21** *Double definition* **23** *Single definition* [Simple reference to 1 *Down*] **24** *Anagram*: nice oils **25** *Hidden word*: Embittered Ralph (*reversed*) **26** *Anagram*: saw knees

DOWN

1 *Double definition* **2** *Double definition* [Overthrows can cause extra runs in cricket] **3** *Single definition* **4** *Single definition* **5** everyone separately = EACH *within* circle = RING **6** politician = MP *within* lie (*anagram*) **7** certain = SURE *after* initial error = E + artist = RA **14** Present = OFFER + conservative [Conservative] = TORY **15** *Single definition* **17** drug = HEROIN + cure finally = E **18** wander *without* direction = ANDER *preceded by* ME **20** Got *reversed* + leg (*anagram*) **22** *Final letters* [tails] *of* Hyderabad, Kashmir, Delhi, Rangoon, Bangkok

PUZZLE 2

ACROSS

1 *Double definition* **9** concerning = OVER + condition = STATE **10** *Hidden word*: trainer tries **11** fashionable = IN + camping equipment = TENT **12** Tree = ALDER + attendant = MAN **13** Initially galloping = G + about = ROUND **15** AS + indicated = SIGNED **18** Trick = CON + attract = TEMPT **19** completely = ALL *inside* holy men = STS **21** Silent = DUMB + signal = BELL **23** A tissue *sounds like* 'Atishoo!' **26** Heather = LING + love = O **27** person initially = P + dwelling = RESIDENT **28** *Anagram*: man so I report

DOWN

1 *Anagram*: rig done **2** *Double definition* **3** *Subtractive anagram*: An ace tenor's *minus* at **4** A girl = 'a lass' (*sounds like ...*) **5** Irritates = NEEDLES + skinhead = S **6** *Hidden word*: piano is excruciating **7** *Double definition* **8** Newspaperman = ED *after* point-to-point = S TO N **14** gold = OR + title = NAME + books = NT **16** eleven (Across) = INTENT + one = I + ON **17** *Double definition* **18** old king (initial letters should be upper case) = COLE *containing* learned religious person = DD **20** steep = SHEER *containing* lieutenant = LT **22** bedroom *without* little Edward = 'Ed' **24** *Hidden word*: selection **25** *Alternate letters*: Immerses

PUZZLE 3

ACROSS

1 Russian = RED + vehicle = CAR **4** *Single definition* **9** *Single definition* [deck = deck of cards] **11** *Anagram*: Merle **12** *Hidden word*: Is he a farmer **13** selling = peddling *sounds like ...* **15** *Hidden word*: need **17** *Single definition* [lights = grid entries] **20** to make a mistake = ERR + IF *within* tide (*anagram*) **21** *Double definition* **23** Verse = CANTO + points = N, E, S, E **25** Strange = RUM + graduate = BA **27** *Hidden word*: mechanised **28** Draw on = INDUCE *containing* rot (*anagram*) **29** *Anagram*: Terns go + South = 'S' **30** Girl = KATE on board, *ie within* SS = steamship

DOWN

1 *Single definition* **2** *Single definition* **3** *Anagram*: a terrific **5** All right = OK *containing* A **6** *Double definition* **7** *Double definition* **8** second-hand = SH + carpets = RUGS **10** better = IMPROVE *containing* IS **14** Disagreement = DISSENT *containing* ID **16** from = EX + stress = TENSION **18** *Single definition* **19** Flags = STREAMERS, *without* river = 'r' **22** fight = SCRAP + sickness initially = S **24** Gangs of witches = COVENS *without* caught = 'c' **26** *Double definition* **28** *Intermittent (in this case even) letters of* filches

PUZZLE 4

ACROSS

1 *Single definition* **10** *Anagram*: Nat is to be **11** old car = BANGER *minus starting letter* **12** Fool = GULL + last letter of silly = Y **13** at = IN + new = N + church = CE *containing* grief = DOLE **14** *Double definition* **16** *Quotation* **18** *Anagram*: twinge containing time = T **20** TO + match = TALLY **21** automobiles without wheels = 'autmbiles' (*anagram*) **23** manner *sounds like* ... **24** Former = EX + deed = ACT **25** A tragic + member = 'MP' (*anagram*) **26** Criminal = CON + going down = DESCENDING

DOWN

2 rude = INSOLENT *containing* advocate's third letter = V **3** *Double definition* **4** organ = EAR *within* part of building = WING **5** *Anagram*: altered **6** *Double definition* **7** *Hidden word*: near gondola **8** Perhaps Latvian = TONGUE + tormentor = TWISTER **9** *Single definition* **15** to instruct = I N I T I A T E + leading driver = D **17** English town = DARLINGTON *without* Head = 'D' **19** Lightweight = GRAM + Manx cat = 'puss' *less* 's' **20** *Subtractive anagram*: generate *minus* R (abbreviation of right) **22** British = BR + eggs = 'ova' *reversed* **23** *Single definition*

PUZZLE 5

ACROSS

1 like = AS + pupil = TUTEE *minus* ecstasy = E **4** *Double definition* **9** *Anagram*: acre **10** Conservative = TORY *after* concert = PROM + in progress = ON **11** disapproval = BOO *containing* A + doctor = MB **12** *Single definition* ['beaten fairly and ...' = roundly beaten] **13** *Quotation* **15** *Double definition* **16** *Anagram*: post **17** *Anagram*: A lame bird **21** Note = B + Queen Elizabeth I = ERI *twice* **22** *Double definition* **24** CIA *containing anagram* Rendell **25** night owls often nap (*first letter of each word*) **26** *Sounds like* earnest. Reference to play *The Importance of Being Earnest* by Oscar Wilde **27** *Anagram*: Master

DOWN

1 Noah's vessel = 'Ark' [a description of which might *sound* old-fashioned] **2** *Hidden word*: towpath robbers **3** *Anagram*: Oil spot **5** *Double definition* **6** *Anagram*: a fleet war **7** Rugby Union = RU + meeting = RALLY **8** Beds = COTS + with = W + ancient = OLD + uplands = HILLS **14** duke = D + routed in (*anagram*) **16** before = PRE + *sounds like* 'Miss' **18** motorway *reversed* = IM + machinery = PLANT **19** the French = LE + husband = GROOM **20** *Hidden word*: the art shop **23** *Double definition*

PUZZLE 6

ACROSS

1 *Double definition* **8** *Double definition* **10** *Double definition* [Brown = surname] **11** headless fish = 'brill' *minus* 'b' **13** Reveals (*anagram*) **15** Hush = SH + rude *sounds like* ... **16** Head [of] gunner = G *changes* to R **17** Grave need made + East = 'E' + Australian = 'A' (*anagram*) **18** Prepare food = COOK + that is = IE **20** swing loosely = DANGLE, D *moves to end* **21** Directions = E, N + police = FORCE **22** back-tracking union = RUN [NUR *reversed*] *containing* one = I **25** *Subtractive anagram*: dim intuition *minus* it **26** Shiite *without* a greeting ['hi'] **27** A dotted line consists of extended = a lot of, dots

DOWN

2 *Hidden word*: Brahmin caste **3** Herb = 'thyme' *sounds like* ... **4** *Reverse direction*: detour *with* 'o' *replacing* u **5** *Double definition* [Read 'Green keeper'] **6** *Initial letters*: Lying upon my back and resting **7** Miss = GIRL + China = FRIEND **9** Team up = ALLY *after* football club = ORIENT **12** Doctor = MB *within* TROON + IS + tense = T **13** *Double definition* **14** *Double definition* **15** Mussolini = 'Duce' (*anagram*) inside emotional pressure = STRESS **19** *Single definition* [colourful way = green] **20** account = ACC + application = USE **23** *Double definition* **24** *Hidden word*: Can one

PUZZLE 7

ACROSS

1 Fool = ASS + one = I *within* company = CO **5** tower = SPIRE *within* part of India = IND **9** *Initial letters*: All clues read over so that I can **10** *Hidden word*: roast enchilada **11** *Anagram*: farm plot **12** IN + church = CH + journalist = ED **13** *Single definition* [American word for normality] **15** *Single definition* **17** *Double definition* **19** *Anagram*: avoids + lines of communication = RY **20** *Substitute* 'e,e' *for first and last letters of* squats **21** *Single definition* ['In the velvet glove ...'] **22** fools = IDIOTS with money = M *substituted for initial letter of* trifles **23** IS + A + beauty = BELLE **24** Late = NIGHT + pilot = FLY **25** unruly children = TERRORS *without initial letter*

DOWN

2 A revolting peasant = A CADE [Jack Cade, one of the leaders of the Peasants' Revolt] *containing* pass = COL **3** wine = PORT *within* shop = SING [criminal slang for inform] **4** DUCK = O + as detour (*anagram*) **5** *Double definition* **6** drug = POT + measure = EN + Cyprus = CY **7** raced = RAN + caught = C + Superman = HERO **8** *Anagram*: die-hard + left = 'L' **14** *Anagram*: Cool cheat **15** BRIAN minus resistance = R *containing anagram*: home **16** Call up = RING *containing* inspiration = MUSE *reversed* **17** *Anagram*: be hearty **18** *Single definition* [Cambridge graduate with first class degree in Mathematics] **19** to = AT + seduce = TEMPT

PUZZLE 8

ACROSS

1 Mineral = MICA *within* mountain pass = COL **5** *Initial letter of* Coleman *substituted for initial letter of* mustard **9** *Single definition* [lord's = Lord's cricket ground] **10** *Single definition* [heavyweight = 'heavy weight'] **11** *Double definition* **13** bearings = S, E S *containing* lock = TRESS **15** *Double definition* **16** Is it permissible = MAY *containing last letter of* auction = N **18** *Single definition* **19** Dashes = DARTS *reversed* + deserted = D + heather = LING **22** *Anagram*: lancing a **23** public money = FINANCE *removing* note = N **25** *First letters*: under frequent observation **26** *Double definition* **28** *Anagram*: sender *containing* title = U **29** Really = INDEED *containing* unknown quantity = X

DOWN

1 Mozart, for example = COMPOSER *removing* right = 'r' **2** *Hidden word*: Bermuda **3** Copper = CU + fit to = ABLE *containing* record = LP **4** old pianist = 'Liszt' *sounds like* ... [old refers to both pianist and solution] **5** *Anagram*: Accurate + directions = 'S,N' **6** *Hidden word*: Rustles up perhaps **7** AT + trial = TEST + state = NATION *without first letter* **8** *Double definition* **12** *Single definition* **14** Engineers = RES + coach = TRAINER **17** *Anagram*: dace + half tiddlers = 'tidd' **18** *Double definition* **20** Greek = GR + relieved = EASED **21** *Anagram*: nice *inside* modern woman = MS **24** Each = PER + one = I **27** *Double definition*

PUZZLE 9

ACROSS

1 Advance payment = SUB + teams = SIDES **5** *Single definition* **10** *Double definition* **11** *Double definition* [stealing a line from — *no hyphen in compound solution*] **12** *Anagram*: danger + Eastern = 'E' **13** *Hidden word*: Baghdad no canard (*reversed*) **15** Complete = 'lot' (*reversed*) *containing* army reserves = 'TA' [Definition is also Complete] **17** *Double definition* **19** *Anagram*: acid near **22** *Single definition* [Reference to 7 Down] **23** *Hidden word*: Tripos term **24** *Single definition* **25** *Single definition* [You might 'set tee' before you drive off in golf] **26** *Double definition* [Ignore comma to read 'Small fleet']

DOWN

1 None *sounds like* 'nun'... **2** *Single definition* **3** fool = IDIOT + in charge = IC **4** *Anagram*: there **6** sailor = AB + breather = REST containing A **7** Endure = STAND + punishment = STOCKS + to the point where = TILL **8** *Anagram*: Duly send **9** *Double definition* [one who's in = batsman; a batsman can take guard on off stump — though this is not usual] **14** rushed over = RAN *reversed* + desert = RAT + gold = OR **16** *Double definition* **18** *Anagram*: tie lent **20** *Single definition* [Cleopatra's life came to a halt because of an asp] **21** PERSIAN *minus* N **23** Two boys = ROY + AL

PUZZLE 10

ACROSS

1 Runs = R *in* fish = TENCH **4** Is old = ART + journal = PAPER **10** *Hidden word*: weather malevolent **11** Girl = MAY + spoken = ORAL **12** again tries = REHEARS + one = I + no good = NG **13** *Anagram*: sink [Reference to 4 *Across*] **15** Suspend = HANG + boxer possibly = DOG **17** Picture = SHOT + set = PUT **19** Problem originating = P + at the back = ASTERN **21** *Anagram*: Roam pie **23** *Double definition* **24** Immediately = STAT + *anagram*: queues **27** note = MINIM + AL [reference to hidden word in answer to 10 *Across*] **28** Knot = TIE + attaches = PINS **29** *Anagram*: Any chits **30** *Single definition*

DOWN

1 Teachers' = TUTORS + joint = HIP **2** *Anagram*: nowhere [Samuel Butler's novel of that name] **3** *Anagram* : recommend a **5** *Anagram*: nice rimes **6** *Double definition* **7** Score = PAR + cut = SNIP **8** *Double definition* **9** *Alternate letters*: see lakes **14** *Double definition* **16** *Anagram*: ITALIAN + for example = EG **18** Stanza = VERSE *within* Arts (*anagram*) **20** *Initial letters*: Spruce, poplar, ironwood, nutmeg, nicotinia, elder, yew **22** Religious Education = RE + old choir = QUIRE **23** Companies = COS *containing* medical graduate = MB **25** *Single definition* [Tate Gallery named after Sir Henry Tate, sugar refiner and philanthropist] **26** *Hidden word*: Martha maybe *reversed*

PUZZLE 11

ACROSS

1 *Single definition* **4 & 2** *Down* Ship's officer = CAPTAIN + Welsh town = FLINT [Long John Silver's parrot in *Treasure Island*] **9** golden rule = 'principle', *sounds like ...* **10** *Last letter of* forms = S + handle = HAFT **11** *Double definition* **12** *Quotation* **13** former = EX + corsair = 'pirate' *less* resistance = 'r' **15** worn = BORNE *reversed* + *last letter of* one = E **17** IN + explosive = TNT *containing* energy = E **19** *Anagram*: a + National Trust = 'NT' + tree (*anagram*) **22** Furnish = PROVIDE + books = NT **24** *Anagram*: resistance unit = 'ohm' + ack-ack = 'aa' **26** *Hidden word*: soprano is exquisite **27** *Anagram*: Take choir **28** *Single definition* [climbers = climbing plants] **29** smoker's accessory = ASH-TRAY *minus* hot = H

DOWN

1 island = CAPRI + church = CE **2** *See* **4** Across **3** Former = EX + chief officer = CO + irate (*anagram*) **4** pass = COL + LATE [Passover = 'pass over', get-together = 'get together'] **5** Dad's = PAS + gratitude = TA **6** Girl = ADA + exercise = PT + fit = ABLE **7** NOT + A + line = RY **8** Work = OP + I + took in = ATE **14** Peter = PAN + TO + act silently = MIME **16** Withdraws = RETRACTS *containing* nothing = O **18** *Anagram*: space to **19** entirety *less* note = 're' **20** Score = TRY *containing* to chase = RACE **21** *Anagram*: Pest in **23** *Double definition* **25** Othello = 'a Moor', *sounds like ...*

PUZZLE 12

ACROSS

1 *Abbreviation of* 'spectacles' *sounds like ...* **5** taxi = CAB *reversed* + vehicle = CAR + to = AT **9** *Double definition* **10** *Hidden word*: metal is sometimes **11** *Single definition* [eye sounds like 'I'] **12** *Double definition* **13** Frenchman = 'M' *contained in* grenade (*anagram*) **15** leads a double life = 'is' *repeated* **17** lavish = 'plush' *take away final* 'h' **19** *Anagram of* REP [salesman] + pain = ACHE + runs =R **20** Measure = EM + device = PLOY **21** a pure one (*anagram*) [Reference to 13 *Across*] **22** Many = M + Ravel (*anagram*) **23** *Double definition* **24** *Anagram*: true saint *without* 'e' **25** *Double definition*

DOWN

2 *Anagram*: a rap song **3** animals = COWS *containing heather* = LING **4** *Anagram*: steer horn **5** *Single definition.* [Reference to Crimean War] **6** *Anagram*: since he [boxer = member of Chinese secret society] **7** Long = L following A + declaration of independence = UDI + is = S + hesitation = ER, overturned [=RESIDUA] **8** Hardy heroine = TESS [Reference to Thomas Hardy novel *Tess of the Durbervilles*] *containing* to approve = AMEN **14** Graduate = MA + to express suspicion = HA + Indian landlord = RAJAH **15** *Single/double definition* [another Crimean War battle] **16** Fashionable = IN + drink = SPIRIT **17** *Anagram*: red paper **18** *Anagram*: ten fauns **19** ONE *within* support = PIER

PUZZLE 13

ACROSS

1 *Double definition* **4** *Single definition* **10** *Double definition* [Louis XV's mistress gave her name to a raised hairstyle] **11** about = RE *enclosed by* mother = DAM **12** soldier = ANT + make private escape = ELOPE **13** *Single definition* **15** *Hidden word*: The aching **17** Put in grave = INTER + appearance = VIEW **20** *Double definition* **21** *Hidden word*: from entrails **24** A + second = S + conveyed = SENT **25** Company = CO + papers = PRESS *containing* Maxwell's initial = M **28** Region = AREA *containing* centre of Genoa = N **29** *Anagram*: cedar tree **30** *Single definition* **31** A + churchman = DD + started = LED

DOWN

1 *Anagram*: parcel Ed **2** Reach = COME + tiptop = T **3** about = RE + League member = ALLY **5** tune = AIR + funny ending = Y **6** *Anagram*: deviates **7** Finished = OVER + with = W + old headgear = HELM **8** TO + atom (*anagram*) **9** *Single definition* [hole sounds like 'whole'] **14** control = REIN + FOR + the Church = CE **16** *Single definition* **18** *Double definition* [Pole = 'pole'] **19** *Double definition* **22** Best start = B + pineapple = ANANAS *less* second = 's' **23** *Double definition* **26** Former = EX + charge = 'toll', *sounds like...* **27** Support = BRA + the = T

PUZZLE 14

ACROSS

1 *Single definition* **8** large sums of money = 'pots' (*reversed*) **10** *Single definition* [Tacky describes tacking, ie going across] **11** a variety of paints = 'oils' (*anagram*) **13** File = LIST *within* information = GEN **15** *Double definition* [Read 'Going up/stairs'] **16** *Initial letters*: Rossini, Offenbach, Nielsen, Debussy, Orff, Schoenberg **17** *Anagram*: a dream has *containing* A + *anagram*: charm **18** *Double definition* **20** refusal = NO + race = TT *within* Kentucky = KY **21** *Anagram*: Paying *containing* quiet = 'p' **22** *Anagram*: Roman *less* article = 'a' **25** Tackle = RIG *inside* cold = C + *anagram*: boiler **26** *Hidden word*: say a mantra (*reversed*) **27** *Anagram*: the saint is

DOWN

2 *Double definition* **3** right = R *within* advice = TIP **4** *Anagram*: Ulster **5** *Single definition* [present = gift] **6** points = E, S, S, E *within* two sides = L, R **7** *Anagram*: truly hopes **9** *Double definition* **12** *Anagram*: fed by prior **13** *Double definition* [Reference to *A Christmas Carol*] **14** *Double definition* ['... Full of sound and fury Signifying ...'] **15** *Single definition* [Reference to syndicate members at Lloyds] **19** *Double definition* [Douglas made an aircraft named after these two states] **20** *Anagram*: Thing + King = 'k' **23** Napoleon's island = ELBA (*reversed*) **24** still = YET + single = I

PUZZLE 15
ACROSS
1 *Historical reference* [Old and Young Pretenders] **6** *Hidden word*: physics laboratory **10** *Initial letters*: often can taste of pretty unpalatable stuff **11** *Literary reference* [Spoonerism: 'nook and cranny'] **12** *Anagram*: river = EXE + trips, + east = E **13** girl's head = 'g' *within* rough = 'rude' [Eponymous hero of Dickens novel] **14** *Anagram*: La Mer **15** *Anagram*: fasts I die **17** loved = DOTED *containing* bird = MINA **20** 'r' *removed from* 'rotter' **21** by *sounds like* 'bye' **23** *Anagram*: a lad r(ight) lung **25** *Double definition* [Indian refers to ink] **26** Beat = TAN + chap = GENT **27** *Double definition* **28** A French = UN + action = DEED *containing* exploit = FEAT
DOWN
1 Soft = P + dress = ROBE **2** *Anagram*: contemplates *taking away anagram of* net **3** Former = EX + fairy = PERI + psychically = MENTALLY **4** *Single/double definition* [DIS = hell. MISS = American waitress] **5** when finally = N + the way up = ASCENT **7** *Anagram* Idle + partner = 'N' **8** Exchange of goods = BARTER *containing* Length of cloth = END **9** *Anagram*: prose concerned **14** *Double definition* **16** *Quotation* **18** directions = E, N *after* drunk = TIGHT **19** river = DEE *containing* RAFT **22** *Anagram*: Knot *containing* end of tie = E **24** *Anagram*: Trade

PUZZLE 16
ACROSS
1 *Double definition* **4** *Anagram*: acres *within* DEED **9** *Single definition* [Snow White should be read 'snow white'; the solution may be thought of as somewhat poetic] **10** exercise = PE *containing* RON [On the contrary refers to indication: clue should read 'Exercise taking Ron'] **11** *Hidden word*: token listening **12** *Anagram*: Treaders **14, 16, 22** *Down*, **29** *Across* **6** *Down Sounds like* story of Waugh [Evelyn] DECLINE AND FALL + about = OF + early Italian group of states = THE ROMAN EMPIRE **16** *See* **14** *Across* **19** *Anagram*: Odes **20** *Anagram*: Wobble *containing* AND + note = 'F' **22** Oddly having lost five hundred = ODLY *containing* debts = IOUS **23** *Double definition* **26** small Italian restaurant = TRAT *containing* one = I **27** levels = STRATA + stone = GEM **28** about = RE *reversed within* tax = EXCISE + *initial letter of* demand = D **29** *See* **14** *Across*
DOWN
1 With Italian = CON + nurse = TEND + Edward = ED **2** *Take away*: trainee = L from succeed = DO WELL **3** *Double definition* **4** cull *substituting* D for 'c' [one hundred + four hundred in Roman numerals] **5** *Single definition* [two = BI (prefix)] **6** *See* **14** *Across* **7** Brief = SHORT + dip = FALL **8** *Hidden word*: cadre a democracy **13** *Anagram*: their slabs **15** one = I inside players' entrance = CAST GATE **17** sound coming from manger = LOW + manger (*anagram*) **18** *Double definition* **21** Brown = RUST + in charge = IC **22** *See* **14** *Across* **24** *Double definition* **25** food = 'bread', *sounds like* …

PUZZLE 17

ACROSS

1 *Single definition* [paid driver] **6** the old way = WISE + right = R **9** *Single definition* [High sounds like 'Hi!'] **10** SHE *containing* 'too' *backwards* **11** *Double definition* **13** *Single definition* **14** Battled = 'fought', *sounds like*... **16** sweetheart = E *within* chap = MAN **17** *Anagram*: such tinted **19** Conservative = C + Bar = LEVER + hesitate = ER **20** readily available = ON TAP. On the contrary ON *becomes* OFF *and* on the contrary TAP *becomes* PAT **23** highly valued = PRECIOUS *containing* company = CO + issue = CHILD **24** *Double definition* **25** *Anagram*: a green + hill = TOR

DOWN

1 Quotes = 'cites' *sounds like*... **2** relevant = APPROPRIATE + point = NESS **3** *Anagram*: the stiff **4** Leader of Hallé = H *within* English Chamber Orchestra = ECO **5** *Anagram*: Enumerate + initial requirements = 'r' **6** *Double definition* **7** *Single definition* [Extremely = at the end] **8** your last = R + bird = EGRET + Edward = ED **12** First of botanists = B + down = UNDER *inside* heather = LING **13** *Double definition* **15** *Double definition* [Description refers to the job of a paid driver] **18** *Double definition* [Reference to Billy Bunter's form] **21** *Single definition* **22** Scottish poet = 'Burns' *without final* 's'

PUZZLE 18

ACROSS

1 *Single definition* ['commonly' has connotation of Commons where members = 'Members' sit] **4** *Anagram*: Crude SAS **10** TO + old pipe (*anagram*) **11** *Hidden word*: Get a citizen's **12** one who adapted music = HOLST + (television) drama = ER **13** *Anagram*: it veers **14** *Single definition* **15** hits back = RAPS (*reversed*) + hits forth (*ie forward*) = TANS **18** *Hidden word*: thunderous sea unusual **20** A + quiet = P + friend = PAL **23** *Anagram*: rig vote **25** *Single definition* **26** *Anagram*: means **27** speech = TALK + Senora Peron = EVITA *reversed* **28** *Single definition* [house = House] **29** present = AD + times = AGES

DOWN

1 *Double definition* [Wagner's opera] **2** old one (chicken) = BOILER *containing* right = R **3** Archer's = TELLS *containing* story = TALE **5** Outstanding = SUPER + of course = NATURALLY **6** consumed = ATE *within* the outskirts of Damascus = D,S **7** *Single definition* [Remove MAN *from the answer to 1 Down* = DUTCH + sale = AUCTION] **8** *Anagram*: Tester **9** cricket's = SPORTS + about = RE + drink = PORTER **16** Prepare = TRAIN + group = BAND **17** *Sparkles* = GLITTERS [Demote, ie one letter earlier in the alphabet, *first letter of* tenor = T to S] **19** *Single definition* [Crewe *sounds like* 'crew'...] **21** suffering = PAYING *containing* right = R **22** First lady's = EVES *containing* not disheartened = NT **24** *Double definition*

PUZZLE 19
ACROSS
1 *Single definition* [Main = connection with sea] **9** *Literary reference* [Darlings' dog in *Peter Pan*] **10** *Double definition* [an 'S' = ans, in other words abbreviation of 'answer'] **11** *Sounds like* HIGH (loud) FIE (blast) **14** *Double definition* **16** *Anagram*: React + partner = 'E' **17** RED *containing* soldier = MAN **18** An extra = 'A leg-bye' (*abbreviation*) **20** *Anagram*: recasts **21** love = O + bites (*anagram*) + may ultimately = Y **22** *Literary reference* [Book title] **24** *Anagram*: Men are **26** Georgia = GA + *anagram*: ate + acceptable = U **27** conservative = C *within* footwear = SANDAL **28** *Double definition* **31** performing = DANCING + nude = 'bare', *sounds like*... **32** Lion family = 'pride' *less first letter* **33** *Single definition*
DOWN
2 *Single definition* **3** gold = OR *within* street = ST **4** hounded = 'chased', *sounds like*... **5** *Single definition* [bridge = bridge of nose] **6** bird = SKUA, *sounds like*... **7** *Single definition* **8** *Miscellaneous* [Sat = 'Saturday' = DAY + IN + sun = 'Sunday' = DAY + abroad = OUT] **12** *Anagram*: Former panel **13** *Single definition* **14** Mists = STEAMS *containing* river = R **15** novel = NEW *within* genuine = REAL **18** *Hidden word*: crevasse **19** *Odd letters*: booty **23** *Anagram*: a pea can **25** *Move last letter of* Claire *to first position* **26** *Subtractive anagram*: arrangement *minus anagram*: meant **29** Lovable girl = MABEL *minus first letter* **30** pub = BAR + key = E

PUZZLE 20
ACROSS
1 Individual = UNIT *containing* student = L **4** oriental = E + woman who is fascinating = WITCH *within* BED **9** *Single definition* [Victory = HMS *Victory*] **10** dog = AIREDALE *minus* bitter = ALE ['perhaps' *refers to both* 'dog' *and* 'bitter'] **11** Not in = OUT + suitable = FIT **12** Leave vehicle = PARK + road = LANE **14** *Single definition* **16** before = 'ante' *reversed* **19** *Anagram*: snag **20** Fluid = WATER + runs = WORKS **22** *Double definition* **23** *Anagram*: A paper **26** *Double definition* [Novel by Graham Greene] **27** Might = MAIN + publish = ISSUE **28** Citrus pith = RAG *inside* European country = FRANCE **29** *Hidden word*: rogue's strategy
DOWN
1 copper = 'd' + turned on (*anagram*) [New is the definition] **2** fast = LENT *sounds like*... **3** hairs growing from ear = TRAGI + about = CA + *initial letter of* lobe = L **4** *Double definition* **5** Licence = WARRANT + that is = IE + partner = S **6** *Anagram*: carts *containing* the middle of Carrickfergus = 'k' **7** I'm present = HERE + in honour of = AFTER **8** *Anagram*: Odd + for example = 'eg' **13** *Anagram*: remain calm **15** *Single definition* [Plate = River Plate, mainly = by the sea] **17** *Miscellaneous* [Solution is combined with 'shock'] **18** Partner = S + somewhere in the East End = WAPPING **21** *Double definition* [Spinner = 'arachnid'; also a long-legged snooker rest] **22** French word = MOT + IF **24** Directions = EN + girl = SUE **25** German wine = 'Wein', *sounds like*...

PUZZLE 21

ACROSS

1 *Single definition* **9** *Anagram*: Might oral **10** No + taxi = 'cab' *(reversed)* **11** *Single definition* [Usually abbreviated to 'ult'] **12** Help = TEND + measure = EN + extremes of company = CY **14** A + *anagram*: canal *containing* cat = TOM + I **16** animal doctor = VET + duck = O **18** *Hidden word*: endorsing evangelism [The gloomy dean in the solution is quite common in crosswords!] **19** *Single definition* [Type of biscuit] **21** *Anagram*: August V [= 5] + Sweden = S **22** *Anagram*: of a gin [Juan Manuel, former world motor racing champion] **25** Not out = IN + US + note = E **26** *Single definition* [board = table] **27** *Single definition*

DOWN

1 Working out = CALCULATING + object of Will's [ie Shakespeare] = MIND **2** Small contribution = 'mite', *sounds like ...* **3** Flash = DART + pad = ROOM *reversed* **4** *Double definition* **5** Moderate = TEMPER + A + northern = N + church = CE **6** foundations = BEDS *following* measurement = EM **7** with Italian = CON *in anagram*: centre **8** *Single definition* **13** *Anagram*: Fires built **15** *Single definition* **17** *Double definition* **20** [Two different words for perform] **23** Country = 'Ghana', *sounds like ...* **24** No = O + *synonym of* **16** *Across*

PUZZLE 22

ACROSS

1 Dismiss = SACK + priests = CLOTH **6** *Anagram*: Beats [Old word for beat] **9** *Hidden word*: latent heat retained [For crucible, read 'Crucible' — theatre in Sheffield] **10** Othello = MOOR + home = IN + mid night = G **11** *Anagram*: inert **12** Counter = BAR + measure = METER *containing* nothing = O **14** *Anagram*: fort *minus* 'f' **15** *Anagram*: as cure's near **17** Eye queue *sounds like ...* IQ **19** Drain = SAP *reversed* **20** *Anagram*: in the gloom *minus* East = 'E' **22** One = I + kind of wood = DEAL **24** *Single definition* **26** *Single definition* [For not intent, read 'not in tent', ie out in the open] **27** Of course = SURELY *minus first letter of* equanimity **28** *Double definition*

DOWN

1 seating *minus* for example = 'eg' **2** *Anagram*: reactor [He with capital 'H'] **3** *Single definition* [For Aspire ... in the City, read 'A spire ... in the city'] **4** about = OVER + position = BEARING **5** Hamlet *minus* allow [= 'let'] **6** *Double definition* **7** small = S + glove = MITTEN **8** Keen = EAGER + Head = NESS **13** *Anagram*: creeps + board = TABLE **14** *Double definition* **16** *Anagram*: Terrier + vet almost = 've' **18** One of the Steptoes = TOTTER *containing* runs = R [The perhaps refers to both definition and subsidiary indication. Reference to TV's *Only Fools And Horses* and *Steptoe And Son*] **19** power = P + start again = RESUME **21** *Anagram*: Italy **23** *Anagram*: Euclid *minus first letter* **25** Gains *minus* 'in'

PUZZLE 23

ACROSS

1 a payment = 'a cost', *sounds like*… **4** *Alternate letters of* raid = AD + project = JUT + soldier = ANT **10** *Single definition* [of the fields in French] **11** *Last letter of* trial = L + recess = APSE **12** to draw = TIE + explorer = POLO **13** on = RE + TAILS *sounds like* tales = stories **14** *Double definition* [Type of hair treatment] **15** *Anagram*: steelmen **18** *Single definition* **20** *Initial letters*: plebeian leaders as top orator **23** *Single definition* **25** *Anagram*: me to her **26** *Single definition* **27** Pointed = E + proposal = MOTION + gangster = AL [Capone] **28** Objectively I = ME + guard = SS + friend = MATE **29** Engineers = REME + defy extremes = DY

DOWN

1 *Single definition* **2** strict order = 'Cistercian' *less* CIA **3** *Double definition* **5** *Single definition* [Orpheus went down to the Underworld = DIS] **6** *Anagram*: until **7** A + soft = P + tip = POINT **8** THE + first = IST **9** *Anagram*: Irishmen vote + Prime Minister = 'PM' **16** *Double definition* [Dam *sounds like* 'damn'] **17** *Hidden word*: [in]form all youngsters **19** *Single definition* [Soldiers = pieces of toast] **21** Called = RANG *within* time = 'era' (*reversed*) **22** Make a killing = 'murder' (*reversed*) **24** *Reverse*: Muesli *less* 's'

PUZZLE 24

ACROSS

1 *Double definition* **4** plant = CRESS + mountain = IDA [Reference to Shakespeare/ Homer/ Chaucer lovers and to 13 *Across*] **10** *Anagram*: Chairs get **11** *Central letters*: D G Rossetti described as **12** *Literary reference* [How they brought the Good News from Ghent to Aix] **13** *Anagram*: lout is *and first letter of* ready = R **14** *Anagram*: Naive **15** *Anagram*: named tea **18** sweets = 'desserts' (*reversed*) **20** Noticed = SEEN *containing* Hancock at first = H **23** *Double definition* **25** old Spanish coin = REAL + looks *sounds like* 'eyes' **26** *Anagram*: tunnel *without last letter of* obstruction = N **27** *Single definition* [Barnstaple is a port in Devon] **28** *Anagram*: foster + line = RY **29** doctor = SURGEON *less first letter*

DOWN

1 *Anagram*: in G Sharp **2** *Double definition* **3** *Double definition* [The – is misleading] **5** *Single definition* [Sinister is connected with the left hand] **6** *Double definition* **7** *Anagram*: Guildenstern *without back* [= 'stern'] **8** donkey = ASS + first = IST **9** Early English king = STEPHEN + profligate = SPENDER **16** *Hidden in abbreviated form in* attendance [TT] **17** *Anagram*: bun + consumed = EATEN **19** *Single definition* **21** Unfinished epic = EPI + novel, for example = TOME **22** Scratch = SCUFF *containing* right = R **24** *Anagram*: Has + OT [part of the bible]

PUZZLE 25

ACROSS

1 *Double definition* **9** *Subtractive anagram*: all over USSR *minus* lovers **10** *Anagram*: River rose **11** *Double definition* **12** *Hidden word reversed*: evil a Klansman **14** left = L *within* regret = RUE **15** *Anagram*: S [= direction] + aggrieves **18** international body = UN + support = STAND *containing* the German = DER **19** *Double definition* **21** *Single definition* **23** *Single definition* [blue, red = corners in boxing match] **25** *Hidden word reversed*: seat a Roman idealizes **26** *Double definition* **27** *Anagram*: Eating rot sister

DOWN

1 *Single definition* [Self-defence in boxing] **2** *Miscellaneous* ['well-' if connected to solution = cosmopolitan] **3** *Single definition* [Latin for on the spot] **4** *Single definition* [plot = garden] **5** Henry = H *replaces first letter of* spraying device = ROSE. Reference to first part of above clue answer. **6** *Anagram*: some girls *minus* I **7** A + European capital = ROMA **8** *Double definition* **13** *Double definition* [Operation] **16** Italian = IT + tanner I (*anagram*) **17** *Anagram*: part + exit = DOOR **20** South African = BOER *containing* doctor = MB [WW2 bomber] **22** A + quantity = MASS **24** cheese = 'Edam' *reversed*

PUZZLE 26

ACROSS

1 Clothing = DRESS *containing* acceptable = U **4** As = QUA + series = TRAIN **10** *Subtractive anagram*: CLAIM HELL IS (hot = *anagram indicator*) *minus anagram of* ILLS (decadent = *anagram indicator*) **11** Drink (*anagram*) + editor = ED **12** *Single definition* [Both climbing plants and employees can be redirected by doing this] **13** cross = 'rood' (*reversed*) **15** supplement = ADD ON *containing* IS [Addison was the original co-publisher of *The Spectator* magazine] **17** directions = EN + count, for example = TITLE **19** *Single definition* [Grey *sounds like* 'Gray', the poet] **21** Scores = TRIES + depleted team = TE **23** *Hidden word*: send up eternal **24** production lacking lines = MIME + on = O + diagram = GRAPH **27** Boy = DICK *containing* stray = ERR **28** mean = CHEAP + measure = EN **29** *Single definition* ['nightlife' *sounds like* 'knight life'] **30** entry = 'ingress', *take away 's'*

DOWN

1 *Anagram* create dam **2** to refer to = CITE *inside* embarrassed = RED **3** Mariner = SEAMAN + is = S + knowledgeable about = HIP **5** *Quotation* [Shakespeare's *Julius Caesar*] **6** Fish = 'tuna' (*anagram*) **7** Broadcast = AIR + left = PORT [where you might view wings] **8** French sculptor = RODIN, reversed **9** 150 = CL + one = AN [reference to 11 *Across*] **14** *Anagram*: Brings neat **16** *Single definition* ['nits' — unwelcome visitors — are sometimes found in children's hair] **18** Brazilian star player = PELE, *reversed* + county = HANTS **20** *Anagram*: Rome, pre **22** knave = SCAMP + king = ER **23** *Double definition* **25** *Initial letters*: exposes all cards held **26** *Reference to 11 Across containing* left = L

PUZZLE 27

ACROSS

1 *Double definition* **6** Accountant = CA + politician = MP **10** *Quotation* ['Men seldom make passes ...' (Attributed to Dorothy Parker)] **11** appropriate to = FOR *inside* hairdo = PERM **12** flower = ELITE *containing* bird = MINA **13** poles = N,S *within* river = DEE **14** *Hidden word*: [part-]time qualification **15** *Anagram*: Hastens + directions = 'E, E' **17** Fertile = GREEN + region = LAND **20** One = I + the French Prime Minister = LE PM (*reversed*) **21** Small girl = DI *within* raced = RAN (*reversed*) **23** A fight = A BOUT *preceded by* prison = STIR [Anglo-Irish word for porridge] **25** *Anagram*: man-eater *minus* 'r' **26** idle = LAZE *containing* here in France = ICI [Definition also part of device] **27** *Initial letters*: sickly and now extremely **28** *Anagram*: Repent in + church = CE

DOWN

1 Keen = 'eager', *sounds like*... [A tidal bore on the Severn] **2** President = P + carte blanche = LATITUDE [American term for cliché is drugstore philosophy] **3** Peter, for example, = 'disciple' [lacking final direction = *minus* 'e'] + IN + heretical = ARIAN **4** to try = TEST + tea (*anagram*) **5** *Anagram*: He pours **7** A seed = A CORN **8** *Single definition, missing letter* [Reference to Scarlett O'Hara, heroine of *Gone With the Wind*. In this clue she loses her foot, not her head. The Scarlet Pimpernel is the eponymous hero of the novel by Baroness Orczy] **9** *Single definition* **14** trains = ENGINES *containing* royal passenger = ER **16** Former = EX + terrorists = PLO + SON *containing* one = I **18** Wind = AUSTER + east = E **19** flyer = BIRD, *reversed* ['high' *indicates reverse direction in a down clue*] + allowed = LET **22** *Anagram* [Reference to solution of 21 *Across*] **24** I (The writer)objectively = ME

PUZZLE 28

ACROSS

1 Fugitive = 'refugee' *minus* direction = 'E' **4** *Double definition* **10** *Double definition* **11** stutterer *minus* way = 'st' *and* royal = 'ER' **12** love = O + lied (*anagram*) **13** End = TAIL + bit = PIECE [Design at the bottom of a page or chapter] **14** *Anagram*: They cared about **18** language = TURKISH + from France = DE + blonde = LIGHT **20** *Single definition* ['box' = hedge] **22** A + fit of bad temper = BATE **24** *Double definition* **25** born = NEE + *anagram*: Sends I [one] **26** Class = FORM + too soon = 'early', *sounds like* ... **27** *Double definition*

DOWN

1 professional = PRO *within* range = REACH **2** mate = FRIEND *minus* partner = 'N' **3** Good Scottish = GUID + publication = BOOK *containing* English = E **5** *Double/single definition* **6** first from the = T + bottom = RUMP **7** Issue = LITTER + concealed microphone = BUG **8** old vessel = ARK *within* study = DEN **9** *Single/ double definition* **15** four out of 6 = TRUM [reference to 6 *Down*] + safe = PETER **16** lecture = TALK + musical = 'Evita' (*reversed*) **17** importance = STRESS + senior journalist = ED **19** *Miscellaneous* [By... = alone] **21** *Anagram*: Eager **23** *Double definition*

PUZZLE 29

ACROSS

1 right = R *within* tent = CAMP **4** *Single definition* [main = 'sea'] **9** *Double definition* [From book by Thomas Hobbes] **10** *Double definition* **11** South African = SA + instrument = LUTE **12** *Anagram*: rehearsing initially = R + no score **14** *Double definition* **16** *Double definition* **19** judge = 'deem' (*reversed*) **20** *Single definition* [naval *sounds like* 'navel'] **22** *Anagram*: Carves + 's, e' [*initial letters of* skiing enthusiasts] **23** *Subtractive anagram*: a trombone *minus anagram of* marten + top = IST **26** Painter = RA + Edward = TED **27** *Single definition* [King Arthur's sword] **28** Old boy = OB + fibbed = LIED *containing* pistol = GAT **29** *Single definition*

DOWN

1 company = CO + deficit = LOSS + *anagram*: Emu **2** *Hidden word*: Devonian village **3** Evaluate = PRICE *containing* some scenes = ACT **4** Such = SO + laughter = HO **5** *Anagram*: Grant only + one = 'i' **6** *Single definition* [bats = 'cricket bats'] **7** effort = 'exertion' (*misplaced letters*) *containing* key = 'C' **8** *Quotation* [*The Ballad of Reading Gaol*] **13** fools = ASSES + street = ST *containing* MEN **15** Three consecutive letters *sound like* EL ['L'] + EM ['M'] + EN ['N'] + totally at the heart = TAL **17** Choose = ELECT + examination = ORAL **18** strange = ODD + spheres = BALLS **21** drink = LAP + follow = DOG **22** Transport = CAR + depart = GO **24** Sad confession = 'I'm blue' *less* novice = 'L' **25** addiction initially = A + detectives = CID

PUZZLE 30

ACROSS

1 City = EC [postal district] + at a standstill = STATIC [transport = transport of delight] **6** domestic duty = 'mopping' *without* page = 'p' **9** a chart = A MAP, *reversed, containing* AN **10** The = T + queen = ER + gunners = RA + safety catch from grenade = PIN **11** young ox = STEER + grow old = AGE **12** Walker = 'rambler' *less first letter* **13** text = 'script' *less last letter* **14** *Anagram*: mental *containing* IN + east = E **17** *Anagram*: near ark I'm **19** *Single definition* **22** French article that = UN QUE *containing* I **23** *Single definition* [Refers to *Book of Revelations*] **24** Greek character = PHI *within* great (*anagram*) [Lead refers to pencil-lead] **25** Brilliant = DEF + article = A + I = ME **26** *Anagram*: firm's first = 'f' + universal = 'u' + rule **27** *Double definition* [American word for decisively beats; also means old records which were made of this]

DOWN

2 tea = CHA + circle = O + citizen briefly = 'cit' (*reversed*) **3** *Anagram*: Great Dani **4** *Single definition* **5** *Single definition* [The ruler, the theme of 4 *Down*, is CATHERINE the Great; mobilized support = WHEELS] **6** *Single definition* **7** disobedient child = IMP + fashionable = U + University = LSE **8** classes = GENERA + hill = TOR **13** *Anagram*: surgeon *containing* councillor = CR **15** maiden = M + *anagram*: a fluster **16** *Double definition* [One definition is given by the answer to 15 *Down* with the third letter promoted by one in the alphabet] **18** *Hidden word*: limit at Entebbe **20** *Single definition* [Count = Dracula] **21** Old trains = BR + not working = IDLE

Help for Themed Puzzles

CHANGING SIDES

ACROSS

1 *Sounds like part of a foot* **5** Intense = DEEP + determined = SET **10** *Playing is anagram indicator* **12** Poke = PROD, *reversed* **13** Thrash = PASTE + general = LEE, *reversed* **16** Variety of *is anagram indicator.* Arabian = AR **17** Fools = GOATS, eating = taking in, 50 = L **19** Girl = LASS *inside* search = GROPE **21** *French word* for coffee + meal = TEA *containing* American state = RI [*The 'in' is the contentious imperative*] **24** (Net) service = LET *inside* sailors = ABS **25** Copper = CU *reversed inside* fast = LENT **26** You = YE + two abbreviations **29** Cold = ALGID, *substitute initial letter of* comfort *for* 500 = D, + fish = IDE ['bringing' *is a link word*] **30** Three abbreviations ['by' *is a link word*] **31** Extravagantly *is anagram indicator.* Father *is abbreviated to* FR **32** First letter of relish + say = EG + MATA [*Reference to* Mata Hari] **33** Eye = EE + *first letter of* lens + *last letter of* photography

DOWN

1 *Anagram of* Hilda + be pregnant = GO. Made *is anagram indicator* **2** Everybody = ALL + loves = OS + A + primitive = UR [*prefix*] **3** Gazelle possibly = ANTELOPE *minus* before = ANTE [*prefix*] **4** Exercises = PE *inside* 60s teenagers = MODS **6** Dissolute *is anagram indicator* **7** Spenser's *indicates Spenserian word*, former = EX + dump = TIP, *taking in last letter of* malodour **8** Initial letters **9** Reported = TOLD, *substitute one abbreviation for another* **11** *French word for* fire + the = T + band = RING **14** *Initial letters of* ravage Indonesians = RI *after* insect = BEE bites, *ie grips* wife = RIB **15** Drink = HALF + to swallow = SHIFT **18** *Single cryptic definition* **20** Note = FA + score = TALLY **22** *Initial letter of* appals, + first rate = AI + bed = COT, *both reversed* **23** Acceptable = U *inside* wooden artefacts = TREEN **26** Hidden **27** Giant = MAGOG *without first letter* **28** Australia = A *inside* tree = ELM, *reversed*

QUADRANTS

ACROSS

1 Spike = EAR + hair = LOCK **2** So much the worse = TANT PIS *minus* conservationists = NT **9** [Post *indicates coming after*] Circuit = NOR + THE + abbreviation **11** *Subtractive anagram.* Transfer *is anagram indicator. It is an &Lit* **13** Smashed *is anagram indicator* **14** *Hidden* **16** Bear = SIT + abbreviation **17** Respectful term = U *substituted for first* I *in* tent = tipi **19** Former sex symbol = BARDOT *minus* abbreviation **22** Pub = INN *inside* thrown = SHIED [Members = arms and legs] **24** Is formed *is anagram indicator* **25** Perhaps evens = ODDS + bet = LAY *minus* appeal = SA **28** Westminster = WI + politician = MP **30** Here = YO + raw recruit = YOB, *minus* abbreviation **32** *Single cryptic definition* [Social worker = ant] **34** Abbreviation + fiat possibly = CAR, *all reversed* **35** *Subtractive anagram. Indicators are* worked *and* intricate **36** *Three initial letters containing two abbreviations* **37** *Initial letter* + is not = AINT **38** Soldiers = REGIMENT *minus abbreviation*

DOWN

1 [Edmund's *indicates Spenserian word*] Caught = KEIGHT *minus last letter of* jack **2** One = A *inside* angler = ROD **3** Dry = TT *inside* row = OAR **4** *Double definition* **5** Transactions = TR + *first and last letters* **6** *Alternate letters* **7** Take = R *inside* anagram; revision *is anagram indicator* **8** [Up north *indicates Scottish word*] Unknown = Y + party = DO + head = BEAN, *all reversed* **10** The German = DER + abbreviation, *inside* letter = EPIS **12** Crude = ROUGH + crayon perhaps = DRAW **15** Journal = J *replacing first letter of* 28 *Across* **18** Look = AIR + abbreviation + river = OUSE **20** Coming to *is anagram indicator* **21** Served = DID + *three abbreviations* **23** UN chief = ANAN, reversed **26** *Last letter of* Hell + *four initial letters* **27** Horses = STRING *minus abbreviation* **29** Try kissing = PREE + *abbreviation* **31** Love = O + with German = MIT **33** Lit *is anagram indicator*

SOMETHING TO WORRY OVER

Clues without definition

Leading player = STAR + Terry *minus* lines = ry = TER

Run = R *inside* fratricide = CAIN

Mug = ROB *reversed, including* former spouse = EX, *reversed*

Easy *is anagram indicator*

Russia *is abbreviated.* Foreign *is anagram indicator*

Sailor = TAR + suspicious behaviour = SUS

Hidden

Appearing in court = UP; first letter R *inside* prison = STIR

ACROSS

10 *Anagram of* Maria *minus first letter* **11** First letter H + in = I + time = ERA + two abbreviations **12** AND + first letter *inside* potter's box = SAGGER **14** *Alternate letters of* tonite **16** Henry = H *inside* name = CITE, *reversed* **19** *Sounds like*: fall = rain = REIN + costly = dear = DEER **22** Railway = EL + A + abbreviation **26** Mother = ma *coming out of what the answer to* 19 *Across is an example of* **27** Explosions = BURSTS *with* iodine abbreviated *inserted at two separate intervals* **30** Contrived *is anagram indicator* **34** Hill Dweller = RED ANT *minus* last letter **35** Double definition **38** Triumphant cries = OLES *inside* old city = TYRE **39** *French word for* to be, *reversed*

DOWN

1 First = IST *in* abbreviation **2** Block = TRANCHE *minus* abbreviation **3** Princess (briefly) = DI *inside* pop music = RAI **4** Broadcast *is anagram indicator* **5** Fair = UPRIGHT + game = EO + (objectively) we = US + head = NESS **6** Could develop into *is an anagram indicator* **7** Violin = STRAD *reversed* **8** Blackcurrant drink = KIR. *Abbreviation for* king *drops down* **9** Unfortunately *is anagram indicator* **13** Somewhere in Bombay = NASIK *reversed* **15** *Double definition* **17** *Initial letters* **20** I + struggled = VIED **21** Batter = RAM *inside most of* a crusty savoury = PASTI(e) **24** *Single cryptic definition* **25** Three abbreviations **28** Popular = IN + pose = SIT + acceptable = U **29** School = SCH + pupil = L + old record = EP **31** Initial letter + one = A + abbreviation **32** King = REX + IS *all reversed* **36** Two abbreviations

JAYWALKING
ACROSS
1 *Double definition* **5** *First and last letters* + *Anagram of* 'lies' **10** ESC + ARP + MEN + T **11** TYRE *with JAP substituted for* Tyr. **12** Q in W + A +F **13** T in JUNO **14** [Reciter of romances + court fool]. *Single cryptic definition.* **16** JAR + WORK *minus* K, *reversed.* **18** ER + GO **19** EX + IT **20** JIMMY *minus* MY (ie unsurprisingly), + P [In Aberdeen *suggests* Scots word] **22** Beam = JOIST, *substitute* N *for* S. **23** AD + JUST. **25** *Single/double cryptic.* JIMJAMS. **30** JAY *no last letter* + SS [Lost *indicates archaic word*] **31** AMY (The aeronaut) + L **32** ARCUS *minus* U **33** JO + UNCE **34** IF + TA *both individually reversed* **36** *Hidden reversed* **37** JUDOGI *minus* GI **38** HIGH + ROLL + RE *reversed* **39** RENNE + T [Once *is archaic indicator*] **40** *Anagram of* press + *first letter* [Of yesterday *is archaic indicator*]
DOWN
1 JADE in BED (*ie retired*) **2** OR (*sounds like* ORE) *reversed* in JASPE + US **3** *Hidden* **4** *Triple definition* **6** A in DEFT **7** JURE in INS **8** *Double definition with archaic indicator. Enter* EAT **9** COW PIE minus IE in SS, (*reference to Beano character*) **12** *Last letters* **15** *Anagram* [To be awkward *is the indicator*] **17** R + IT **21** *Anagram* of ROSE SCREAMED *minus* ROSA **23** AMMON *minus last letter* **24** F *in* KAFIR **25** S *in* IO **26** MARTINI *minus* I [*ie* drink dropping in (= I) for flier] **27** *Reference to the actor.* LUNA *with* A *moved to the top* **28** MAN + GLEG *minus last letter* [*The Scotsman's indicates Scottish word. Supporting indicates beneath in a down clue*] **29** CORTES *with* ES *moved to the top* **31** EGAD + A *reversed* **33** BOARS *minus* B **35** VI *reversed in* JE

Solutions

It is standard practice with puzzle solutions not to indicate word divisions. We have, however, given hyphens, which are shown by a short bar between one square and the next.

Spelling conventions are always determined by the structure of the clue: the setters must ensure that any solution with variant spellings is clued so that only one of the variants is correct. Note that in our own puzzles, the variant -ize is generally used (in a word such as REALIZE); you will find, however, that puzzles in daily papers prefer mainly the -ise variant (REALISE), which is easier to clue, especially in anagrams.

The solution grids to the themed puzzles containing amended lights show the final version required, followed by a list of answers before amendment.

CROSSWORD NO. 1

CROSSWORD NO. 2

CROSSWORD NO. 3

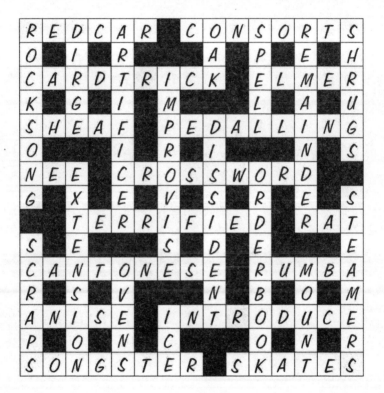

CROSSWORD NO. 4

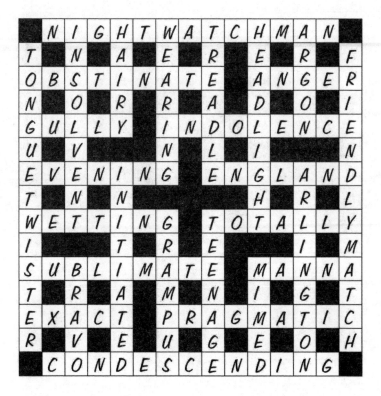

CROSSWORD NO. 5

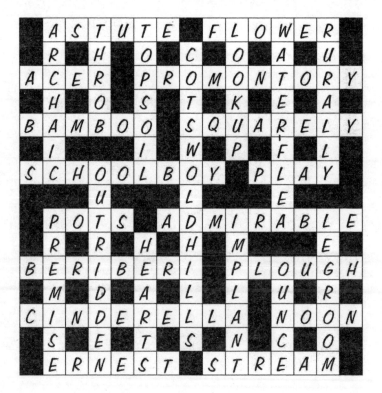

CROSSWORD NO. 6

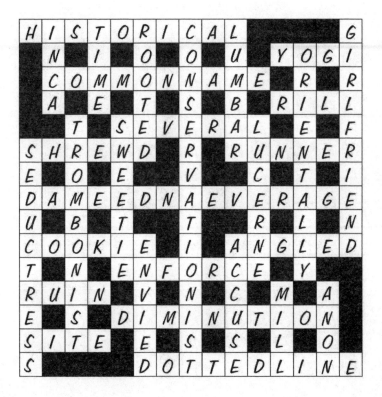

CROSSWORD NO. 7

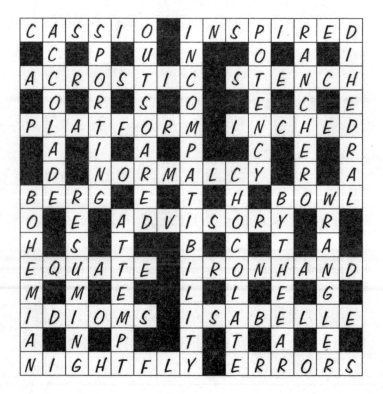

CROSSWORD NO. 8

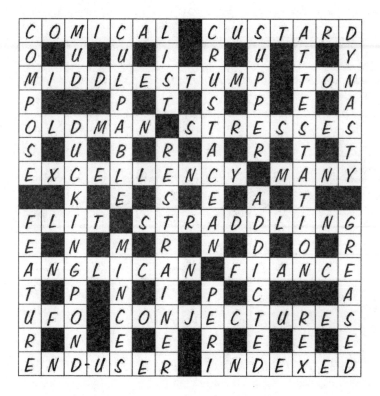

The completed crossword grid reads:

C	O	M	I	C	A	L		C	U	S	T	A	R	D
O		U		U		I		R		U		T		Y
M	I	D	D	L	E	S	T	U	M	P		T	O	N
P			P		T		S		P		E		A
O	L	D	M	A	N		S	T	R	E	S	S	E	S
S		U		B		R		A		R		T		T
E	X	C	E	L	L	E	N	C	Y		M	A	N	Y
	K		E		S		E		A		T	
F	L	I	T		S	T	R	A	D	D	L	I	N	G
E		N		M		R		N		D		O		R
A	N	G	L	I	C	A	N		F	I	A	N	C	E
T		P		N		I		P		C			A
U	F	O		C	O	N	J	E	C	T	U	R	E	S
R		N		E		R		E		E		E
E	N	D-U	S	E	R		I	N	D	E	X	E	D

155

CROSSWORD NO. 9

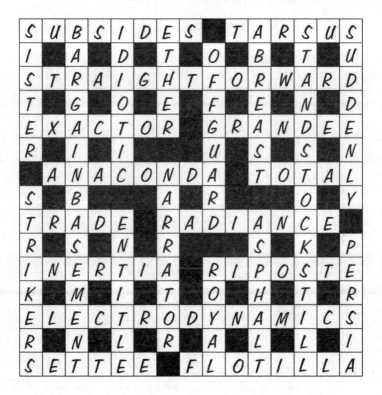

CROSSWORD NO. 10

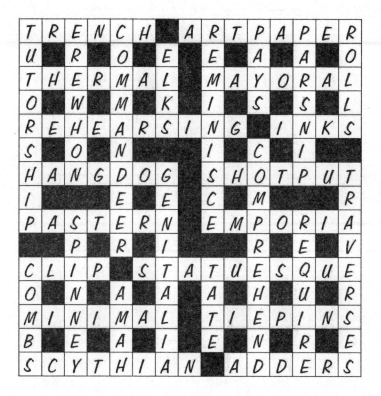

The completed crossword grid reads:

Row 1: T R E N C H ▪ A R T P A P E R
Row 2: U ▪ R ▪ O ▪ E ▪ E ▪ A ▪ A ▪ O
Row 3: T H E R M A L ▪ M A Y O R A L
Row 4: O ▪ W ▪ M ▪ K ▪ I ▪ S ▪ S ▪ L
Row 5: R E H E A R S I N G ▪ I N K S
Row 6: S ▪ O ▪ N ▪ ▪ I ▪ C ▪ I ▪
Row 7: H A N G D O G ▪ S H O T P U T
Row 8: I ▪ ▪ E ▪ E ▪ C ▪ M ▪ ▪ R
Row 9: P A S T E R N ▪ E M P O R I A
Row 10: ▪ P ▪ R ▪ I ▪ ▪ R ▪ E ▪ V
Row 11: C L I P ▪ S T A T U E S Q U E
Row 12: O ▪ N ▪ A ▪ A ▪ H ▪ U ▪ R
Row 13: M I N I M A L ▪ T I E P I N S
Row 14: B ▪ E ▪ A ▪ I ▪ E ▪ N ▪ R ▪ E
Row 15: S C Y T H I A N ▪ A D D E R S

157

CROSSWORD NO. 11

CROSSWORD NO. 12

CROSSWORD NO. 13

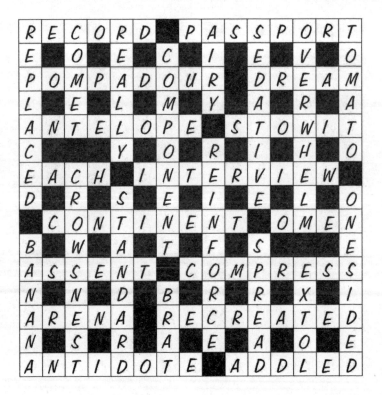

CROSSWORD NO. 14

CROSSWORD NO. 15

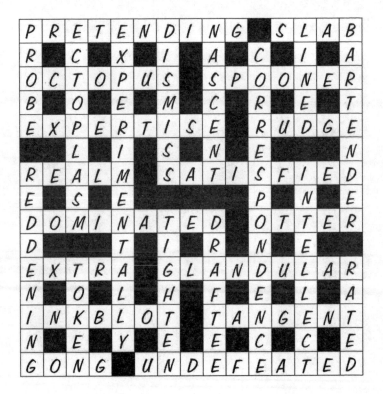

CROSSWORD NO. 16

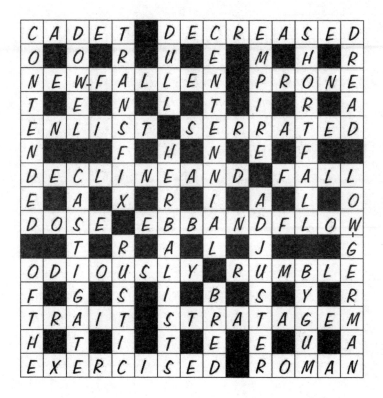

CROSSWORD NO. 17

The completed crossword grid reads:

Row 1: CHAUFFEUR ▪ WISER
Row 2: I ▪ P ▪ I ▪ C ▪ E ▪ O ▪ T ▪ E
Row 3: TOPOFTHEMORNING
Row 4: E ▪ R ▪ T ▪ O ▪ U ▪ K ▪ C ▪ R
Row 5: SOOTHE ▪ UNBUCKLE
Row 6: ▪ P ▪ S ▪ B ▪ E ▪ P ▪ T ▪ T
Row 7: CARDEALERS ▪ FORT
Row 8: O ▪ I ▪ T ▪ U ▪ A ▪ S ▪ T ▪ E
Row 9: MEAN ▪ UNSTITCHED
Row 10: I ▪ T ▪ R ▪ D ▪ E ▪ A ▪ E ▪
Row 11: CLEVERER ▪ OFFPAT
Row 12: S ▪ N ▪ M ▪ R ▪ B ▪ F ▪ O ▪ U
Row 13: PRECOCIOUSCHILD
Row 14: O ▪ S ▪ V ▪ N ▪ R ▪ A ▪ N ▪ O
Row 15: TASTE ▪ GENERATOR

CROSSWORD NO. 18

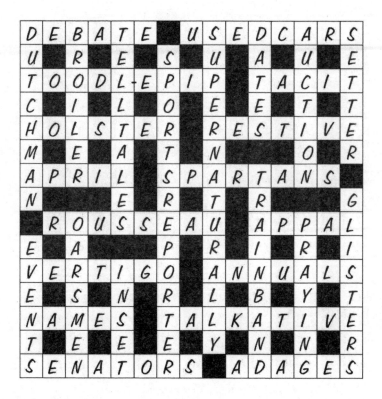

CROSSWORD NO. 19

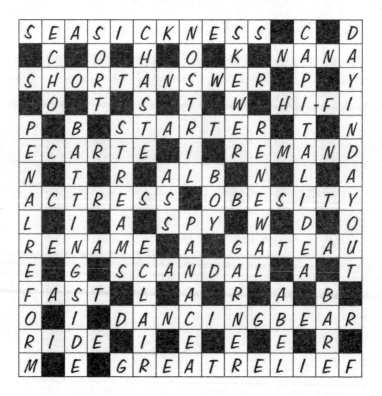

CROSSWORD NO. 20

CROSSWORD NO. 21

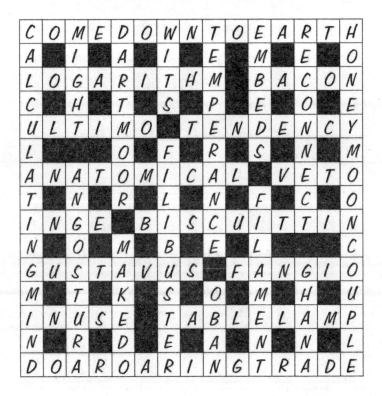

CROSSWORD NO. 22

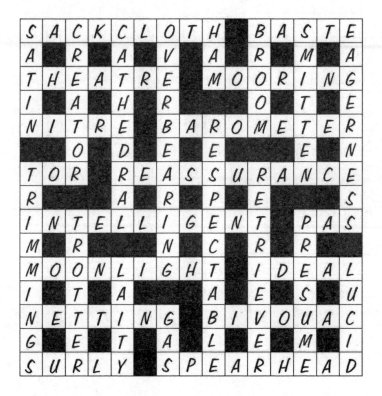

CROSSWORD NO. 23

A	C	C	O	S	T		A	D	J	U	T	A	N	T
U		I		C		I		I		N		P		H
D	E	S	C	H	A	M	P	S		L	A	P	S	E
I		T		O		P		O		I		O		I
T	I	E	P	O	L	O		R	E	T	A	I	L	S
O		R		N		V		I				N		T
R	I	N	S	E		E	L	E	M	E	N	T	S	
S			R		R		N		X					F
	T	E	E	S	H	I	R	T		P	L	A	T	O
R		G			S		A		L		R			R
E	N	G	L	I	S	H		T	H	E	O	R	E	M
D		C		L		M		I		T		A		A
R	O	U	G	E		E	M	O	T	I	O	N	A	L
U		P		U		N		V		N		G		L
M	E	S	S	M	A	T	E		R	E	M	E	D	Y

CROSSWORD NO. 24

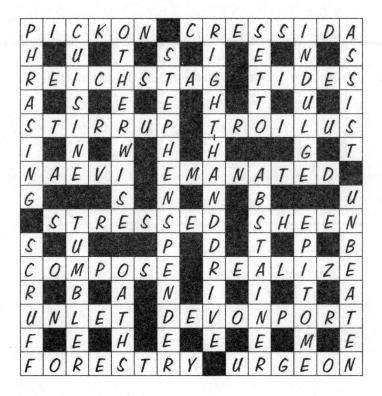

P	I	C	K	O	N		C	R	E	S	S	I	D	A
H		U		T		S		I		E		N		S
R	E	I	C	H	S	T	A	G		T	I	D	E	S
A		S		E		E		H		T		U		I
S	T	I	R	R	U	P		T	R	O	I	L	U	S
I		N		W		H		H			G			T
N	A	E	V	I		E	M	A	N	A	T	E	D	
G			S		N		N		B				U
	S	T	R	E	S	S	E	D		S	H	E	E	N
S		U			P		D		T		P		B
C	O	M	P	O	S	E		R	E	A	L	I	Z	E
R		B		A		N		I		I		T		A
U	N	L	E	T		D	E	V	O	N	P	O	R	T
F		E		H		E		E		E		M		E
F	O	R	E	S	T	R	Y		U	R	G	E	O	N

CROSSWORD NO. 25

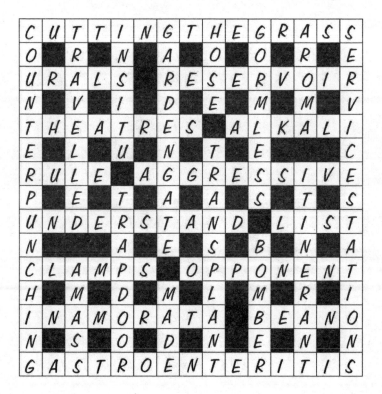

C	U	T	T	I	N	G	T	H	E	G	R	A	S	S
O		R		N		A		O		O		R		E
U	R	A	L	S			R	E	S	E	R	V	O	I	R
N		V		I		D		E		M		M		V
T	H	E	A	T	R	E	S		A	L	K	A	L	I
E		L		U		N		T		E				C
R	U	L	E		A	G	G	R	E	S	S	I	V	E
P		E		T		A		A		S		T		S
U	N	D	E	R	S	T	A	N	D		L	I	S	T
N				A		E		S		B		N		A
C	L	A	M	P	S		O	P	P	O	N	E	N	T
H		M		D		M		L		M		R		I
I	N	A	M	O	R	A	T	A		B	E	A	N	O
N		S		O		D		N		E		N		N
G	A	S	T	R	O	E	N	T	E	R	I	T	I	S

CROSSWORD NO. 26

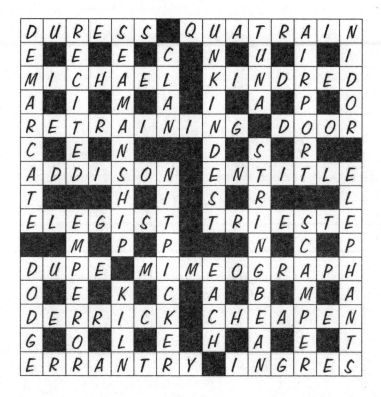

CROSSWORD NO. 27

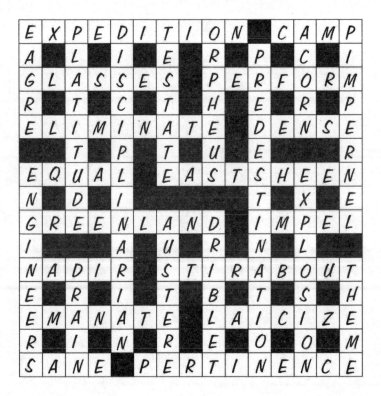

CROSSWORD NO. 28

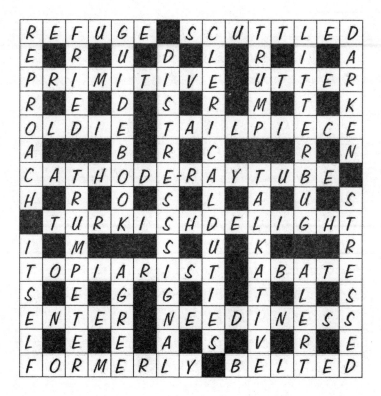

CROSSWORD NO. 29

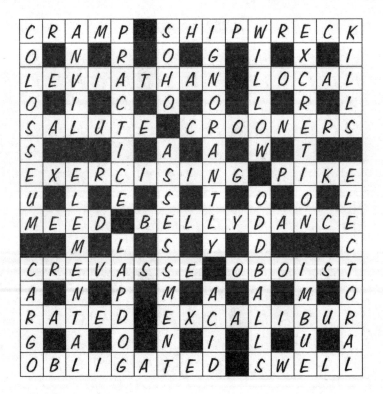

CROSSWORD NO. 30

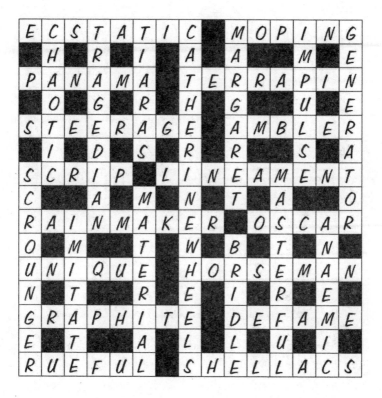

CHANGING SIDES by Gander

H	E	A	R	M	D	E	E	P	S	E	T
I	B	R	O	O	D	A	X	E	K	F	O
D	O	R	P	P	A	S	T	E	E	E	R
A	B	O	E	E	H	Y	I	L	O	U	T
R	E	S	E	D	A	G	R	O	A	T	S
G	R	A	S	S	R	O	P	E	X	R	F
O	I	U	C	A	F	E	T	E	R	I	A
A	B	R	E	T	S	R	U	C	E	N	T
Y	E	A	H	O	H	S	R	M	T	G	A
A	R	G	I	C	I	D	E	A	R	A	R
R	I	O	D	I	F	F	E	R	E	D	R
R	E	G	M	A	T	A	N	E	E	R	Y

The unclued light is LOUT, indicating 'left out'. All other Ls in answers must be changed to Rs, as indicated by the highlighted diagonal giving the alternative title.

Affected solutions are: Across: 1, 10, 13, 17, 19, 24, 25, 29, 30, 33 Down: 1, 2, 3, 9, 15, 18, 20, 26, 28

QUADRANTS by Mordred

W	A	R	L	O	C	K	T	A	P	I	N
I	N	O	R	T	H	E	R	L	Y	E	A
G	R	A	N	T	O	R	E	O	L	P	E
H	O	D	J	A	W	I	T	H	O	I	B
T	U	P	I	R	C	A	B	A	R	D	O
T	G	D	M	W	H	I	N	N	I	E	D
S	H	I	P	W	O	R	M	A	C	R	Y
O	D	D	L	Y	W	H	S	S	I	M	P
U	R	I	Y	O	Y	O	T	A	P	I	R
R	A	C	A	M	S	U	R	B	A	S	E
I	W	O	M	I	S	S	I	B	L	E	E
S	A	I	S	T	R	E	G	I	M	E	S

In each quadrant of the completed grid, NE, NW, SE and SW, only the appropriate
quadrant letters must appear. Thus S and W do not appear in the NE quadrant.
Note the letters in the two diagonal squares in each corner. Affected solutions are:

Across:

1 EARLOCK becomes WARLOCK
2 TAPIS becomes TAP IN
16 SITH becomes WITH
22 SHINNIED becomes WHINNIED
28 WIMP becomes SIMP
37 SAINT becomes SAIST
38 REGIMEN becomes REGIMES

Down:

1 EIGHT becomes WIGHT
23 NANA becomes NASA
29 PREEN becomes PREES

SOMETHING TO WORRY OVER by Mordred

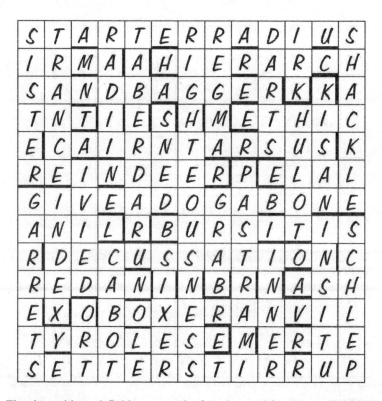

The clues without definitions comprise four dogs and four bones: STARTER, CAIRN, BOXER, SETTER, and RADIUS, TARSUS, ANVIL, STIRRUP. The unclued light, indicating method of entry is: GIVE A DOG A BONE.

JAYWALKING by Mordred

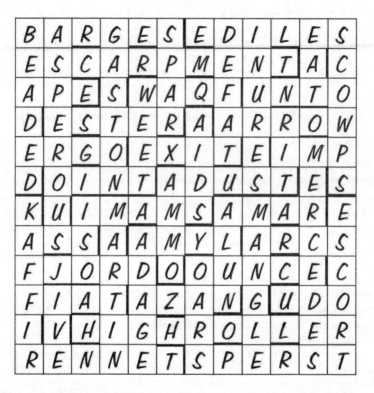

B	A	R	G	E	S	E	D	I	L	E	S
E	S	C	A	R	P	M	E	N	T	A	C
A	P	E	S	W	A	Q	F	U	N	T	O
D	E	S	T	E	R	A	A	R	R	O	W
E	R	G	O	E	X	I	T	E	I	M	P
D	O	I	N	T	A	D	U	S	T	E	S
K	U	I	M	A	M	S	A	M	A	R	E
A	S	S	A	A	M	Y	L	A	R	C	S
F	J	O	R	D	O	O	U	N	C	E	C
F	I	A	T	A	Z	A	N	G	U	D	O
I	V	H	I	G	H	R	O	L	L	E	R
R	E	N	N	E	T	S	P	E	R	S	T

This puzzle is a pangram. The letter 'J' has been omitted from all clued answers before their entry into the grid. Resultant entries are all real words. The unclued lights are AMAR, or JAMJAR before treatment, and FJORD, or FORD before J has walked into it. JAMJAR is rhyming slang for CAR. The following can be found in the completed grid: CAR (in ESCARPMENT), IMP, FIAT, ROLLER, KA, ASTON MARTIN, MERCEDES and ESCORT.

Further Reading and Contacts

Recommended Dictionaries

For most crossword enthusiasts, *The Chambers Dictionary* is the recommended single-volume reference. It contains an enormous number of words not to be found in most other dictionaries and is essential for those wishing to progress to really advanced cryptic puzzles. It also has very useful abbreviations and supplements, eg first names. The only disadvantage of *Chambers* is that it does not contain many encyclopedic entries. *Collins English Dictionary* and *The New Oxford Dictionary of English* each contain a useful number of proper names. The former is the standard dictionary for the daily puzzle in *The Times*. *Chambers Crossword Dictionary* and *Bradford's Crossword Solver's Dictionary* are also very useful.

Other Reference Sources

An atlas such as *The Times Concise Atlas* is useful, as is *Brewer's Dictionary of Phrase and Fable* (Cassell) — a mine of recondite information. An important means of solving literary clues is a quotation dictionary: *The Oxford Dictionary of Quotations* is the most widely recommended. A thesaurus can be very useful — the original is the thematic *Roget's* (Penguin publish this in paperback).

Crossword 'Cribs'

Never be ashamed of using these: all the setters do! There are a lot available: Chambers publish *Anagrams*, *Back-Words*, and the *Crossword Completer*. The last-mentioned lists words from 4 to 15 letters long, alphabetically arranged in order of alternate letters, to allow the crossword solver to complete a solution from the letters already filled in on a grid. Another useful crossword reference is *The Complete Crossword Companion* by Jeremy Howard-Williams (Grafton).

Books on Crosswords

Unfortunately, many of the classic works are out of print. Still available is *Ximenes on the Art of the Crossword* by D S Macnutt, recently republished by Swallowtail Books — one of the definitive books on cryptics. The most complete introduction and guide to both 'standard' and advanced cryptics is Don Manley's *Chambers Crossword Manual*, and a revised edition is now available.

Crossword Clubs

For the real enthusiast, there is the Crossword Club. Their monthly magazine *Crossword* contains tough puzzles and interesting features. Details from: Brian Head, Editor, Coombe Farm, Coombe Lane, Awbridge, Romsey, Hants SO51 0HN.

The Internet

If you search the Internet for 'crosswords' you find hundreds of thousands of sites — certainly enough to keep you busy! One of the best of these is Derek Harrison's *The Crossword Centre* (www.crossword.org.uk). Here you will find a message board; puzzles by Apex, Araucaria, Azed, Ximenes and others; recommendations for books; small ads and much more.

Common Abbreviations
and Clue Equivalents

A	note
AB	seaman
AC	current, account
ACE	expert
AD	advertisement, nowadays
AG	silver
AI	(= A1) first class
B	black, born, bowled, note
BA	graduate, scholar
BR	railway, trains
C	about, caught, Conservative, note
CA	about, accountant
CE	church, engineer
CH	child, church, companion
CIA	spies
CO	care of, Commanding Officer, company
CR	credit
CU	copper
D	dead, died, many, note, (old) penny
DA	District Attorney
DD	churchman
DI	Diana, princess
DR	doctor
E	East, energy, note
EA	each, water
EC	City
ED	journalist
EG	for example/instance
EP	disc, (old) record
ER	queen
EX	former, once
F	fellow, loud, note
FE	iron
FF	very loud

FO	airman
FR	father, France
G	girl, gramme, note
GG	horse
GI	(American) soldier
H	hard, hospital, hydrogen
HE	ambassador, explosive
HP	never-never
HR	hour
I	island, Italy
IC	in charge (of)
IE	that is, that's
II	side, team (=11)
IN	(at) home, fashionable
IS	island
IT	Italian, sex appeal
K	constant, king, thousand
KO	kick off, knock out
L	lake, learner, left, Liberal, novice, pound
LAB	Labour
LB	pound
LP	disc, record
LT	lieutenant
M	maiden, male, many, married, masculine
MA	graduate, scholar
MB	doctor
MD	doctor
MO	doctor, second
MP	Member (of Parliament), politician
MS	(hand)writing
N	North, pole
NB	note
NE	bearing, north-east
NI	Northern Ireland
NO	not out, number
NT	books

NW	bearing, north-west
NY	New York
O	duck, love, nil, nothing, zero
OK	all right
OP	work
OS	extra large, outsize, sailor
OT	books
OZ	Australia, ounce
P	page, parking, penny, piano, soft(ly)
PC	copper, policeman
PE	exercises
PER	ea, for each
PM	afternoon, Prime Minister
PP	pianissimo, pages
PR	price, public relations
PS	afterthought, second thoughts
PT	training
Q	queen, question
R	king, queen, right, river
RA	artillery, artist, gunners
RD	road
RE	about, note
REP	salesman
REV	vicar
RM	jolly, (Royal) Marine
RN	fleet
RR	bishop
RT	right
RU	Rugby Union
RY	lines, railway
S	pole, Saint, South(ern)
SA	army, sex appeal
SE	direction, south-east
SP	betting, odds
SS	saints, vessel
ST	good man, saint, street
T	square, time
TA	army, thanks
TT	non-drinker, (bike) race, teetotal

U	(socially) acceptable, universal, upper class
UK	United Kingdom
UN	a French
US	America(n), useless
V	against, versus
VOL	volume
W	West(ern), wife
X	cross, kiss
XI	players, side
Y	yard, year
YR	year
Z	zero

Roman Numerals

I	one
II	two
III	three
IV	four
V	five
VI	six
VII	seven
VIII	eight
IX	nine
X	ten
XI	eleven
XV	fifteen
L	fifty
C	hundred
CC	two hundred
D	five hundred
M	thousand
MD	fifteen hundred
MM	two thousand

Key to Clue Types and Devices

a   Double or multiple definitions

b   Single definition

c   Anagram:
      i) Simple
      ii) Complex
      iii) Subtractive

d   Split

e   Sandwich

f   Takeaway sandwich

g   Reverse direction

h   Hidden word

i   Sound effects

j   Takeaway

k   Moving letter

l   Substituted letter

m Alternate letters

n   Letter positions
      i) Initials or last letters only
      ii) Only specifically placed letters

o   Abbreviations, numbers and symbols

p   Misleading punctuation
      i) Misleading marks or absence of them
      ii) Running words together or falsely separating them
      iii) False upper or lower case letters

q   Literary, historical or artistic references

r   Reference to another clue

s   Archaic indicator

t   Miscellaneous

u   Definition part of device

Detailed explanations appear on pages 3–12